High Shelf

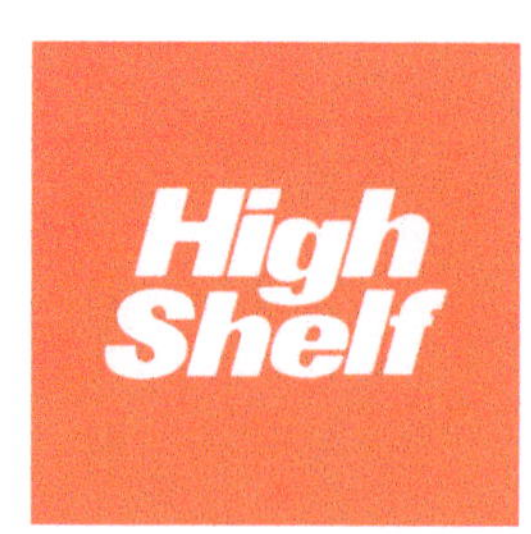

High Shelf XXXI. June 2021.
Portland, Oregon.
Copyright 2021, High Shelf Press

ISBN: 978-1-952869-34-1

Cover Image by Birdee
Design and Layout by C. M. Tollefson
Editing by David Seung & C. M. Tollefson

With special thanks to:
Eric Hoskins, Megan Kim, & River Elizabeth Hall.

High Shelf XXXI

June 2021

"... Look how it becomes nothing
when you forget what you had recognized... "
Leanne Hoppe

"... how quickly she gives away July

so confident that many are still
coming, another year and another.
A book with pages yet to turn..."
Susan DiPronio

Table Of Contents

Last Good Run

Gina Williams

Scent of spawn seeped upstream,
all the way to the city, pulled us blinking,
sand-eyed from winter sleep & we were ready

with nets, buckets, knives.
Gramps cursed his way into icy rush,
green waders gripping river rock by memory.

I paced the shore, skipped stones, puffed cloud breaths.
Gulls ghosted the beach like beggars—
Cowlitz river churning toward tides, black pools alive with catch.

I'd only cut my lip before and maybe scraped a knee
but the mineral smell of blood in the tiny trailer sink,
flash of knives—eggs and guts spilt from slit silver bellies

somehow felt familiar then, made me feel strangely
grown up and wise—falsely so I now understand,
those ancient smelt runs

and Gramps—

gone.

Numbered Not Named

K.G. Ricci

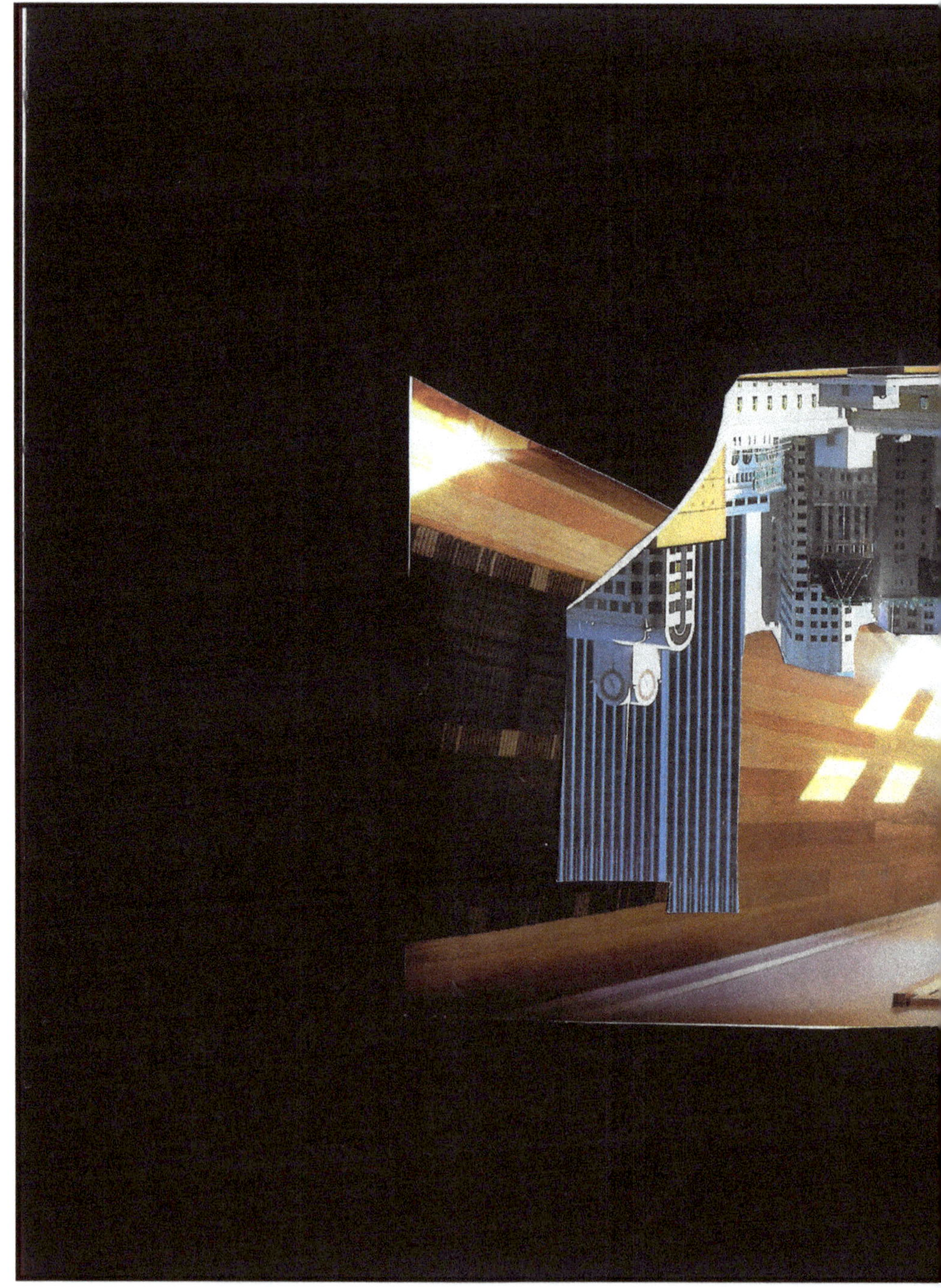

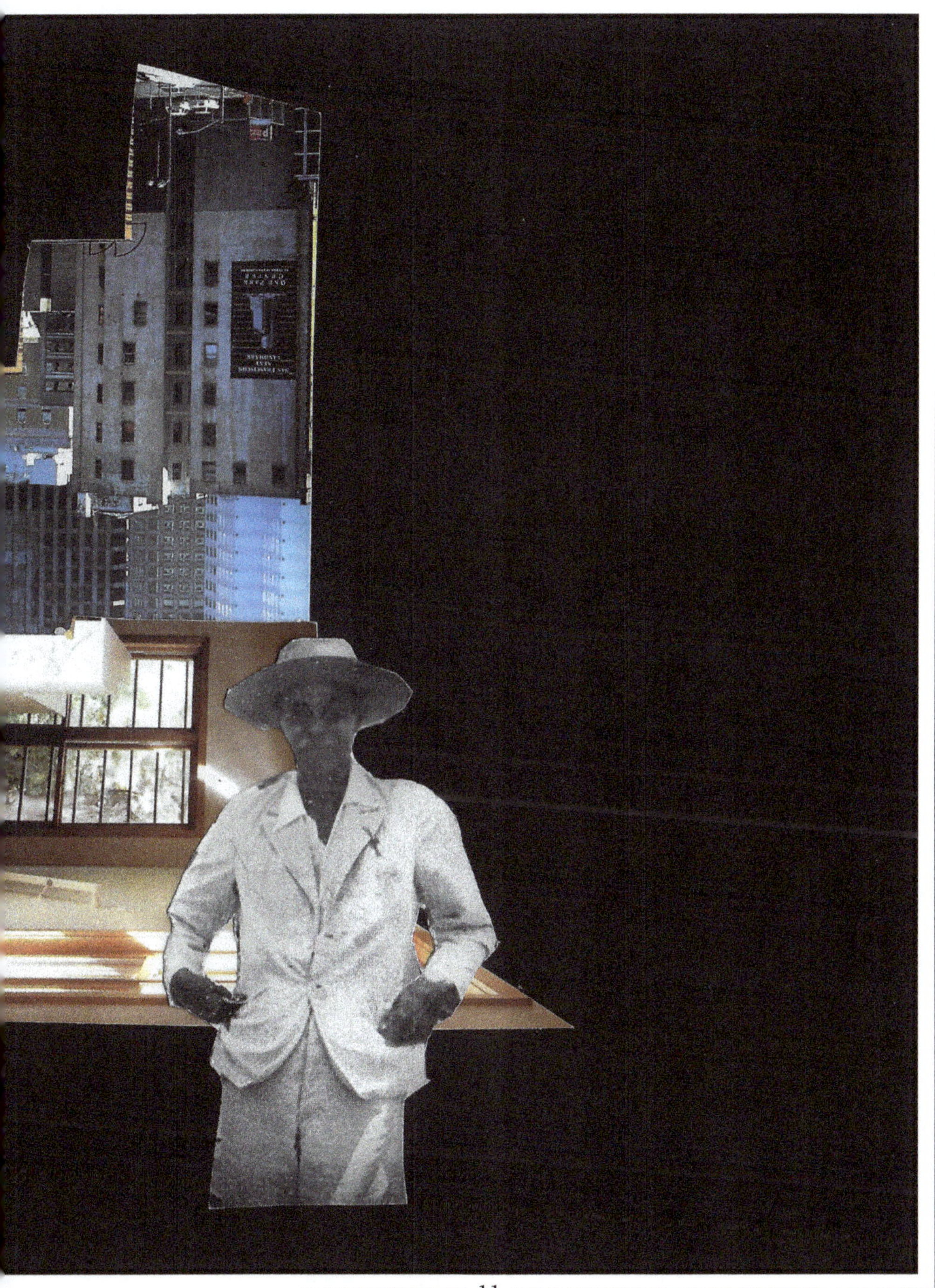

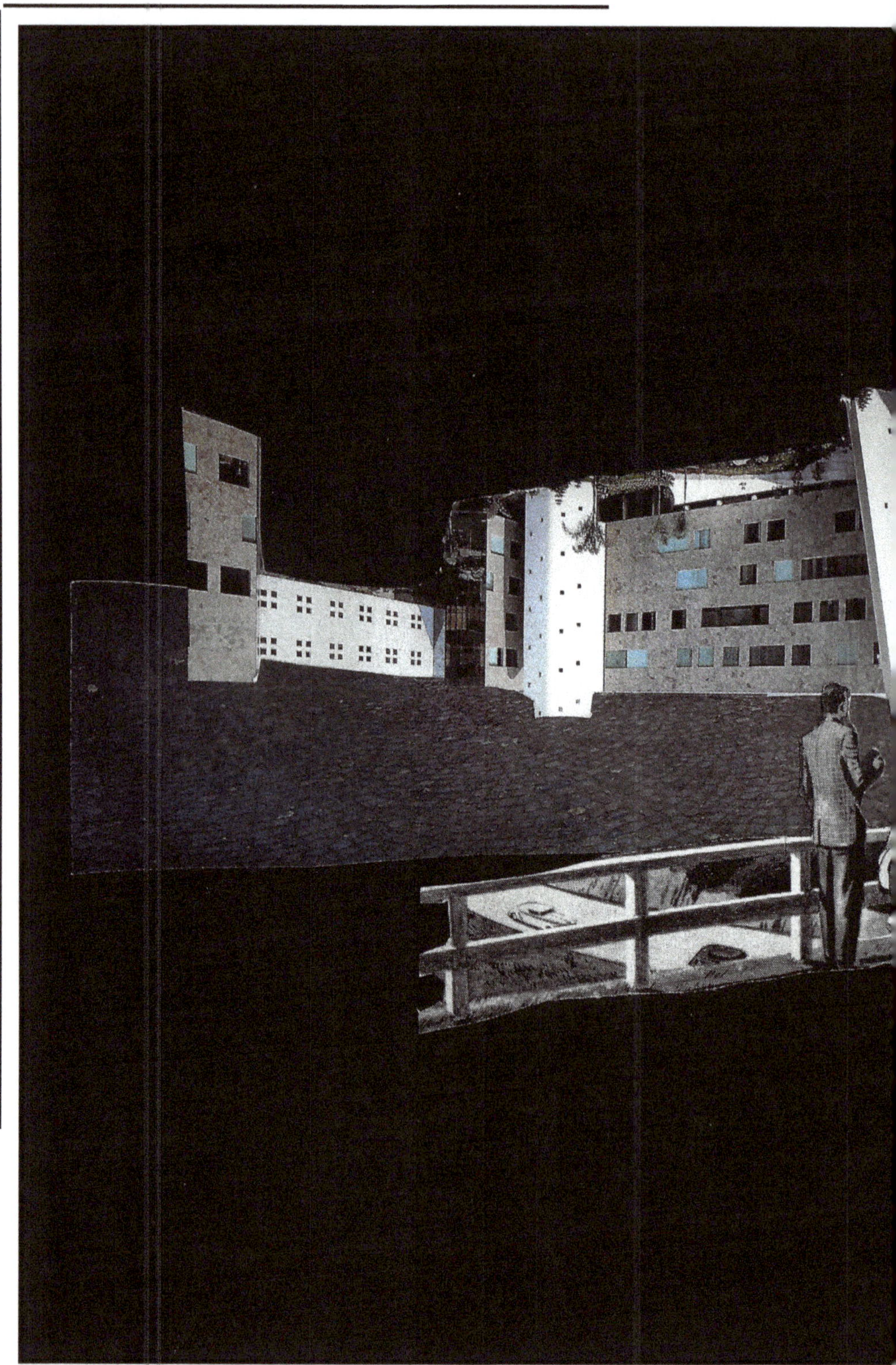

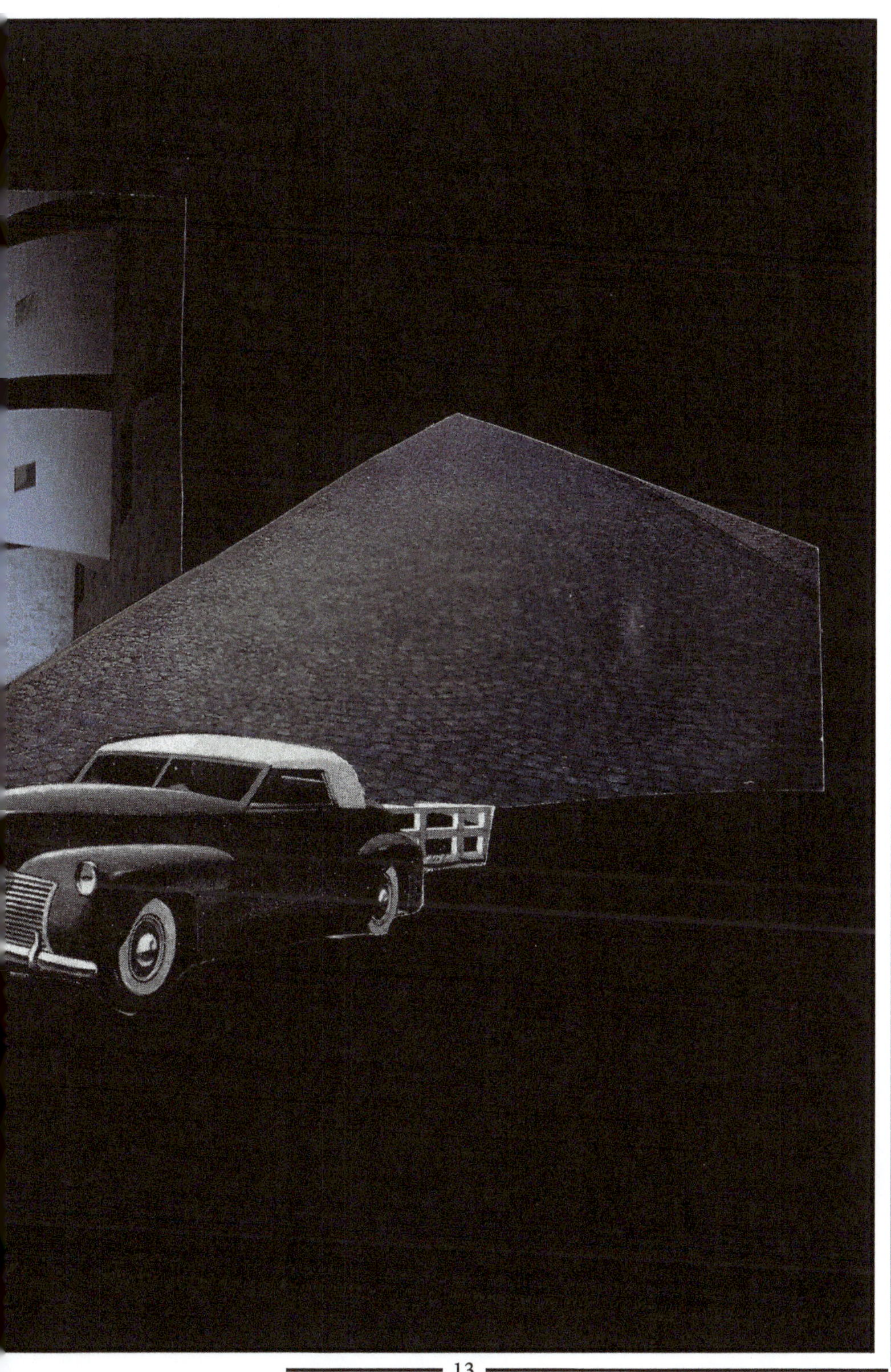

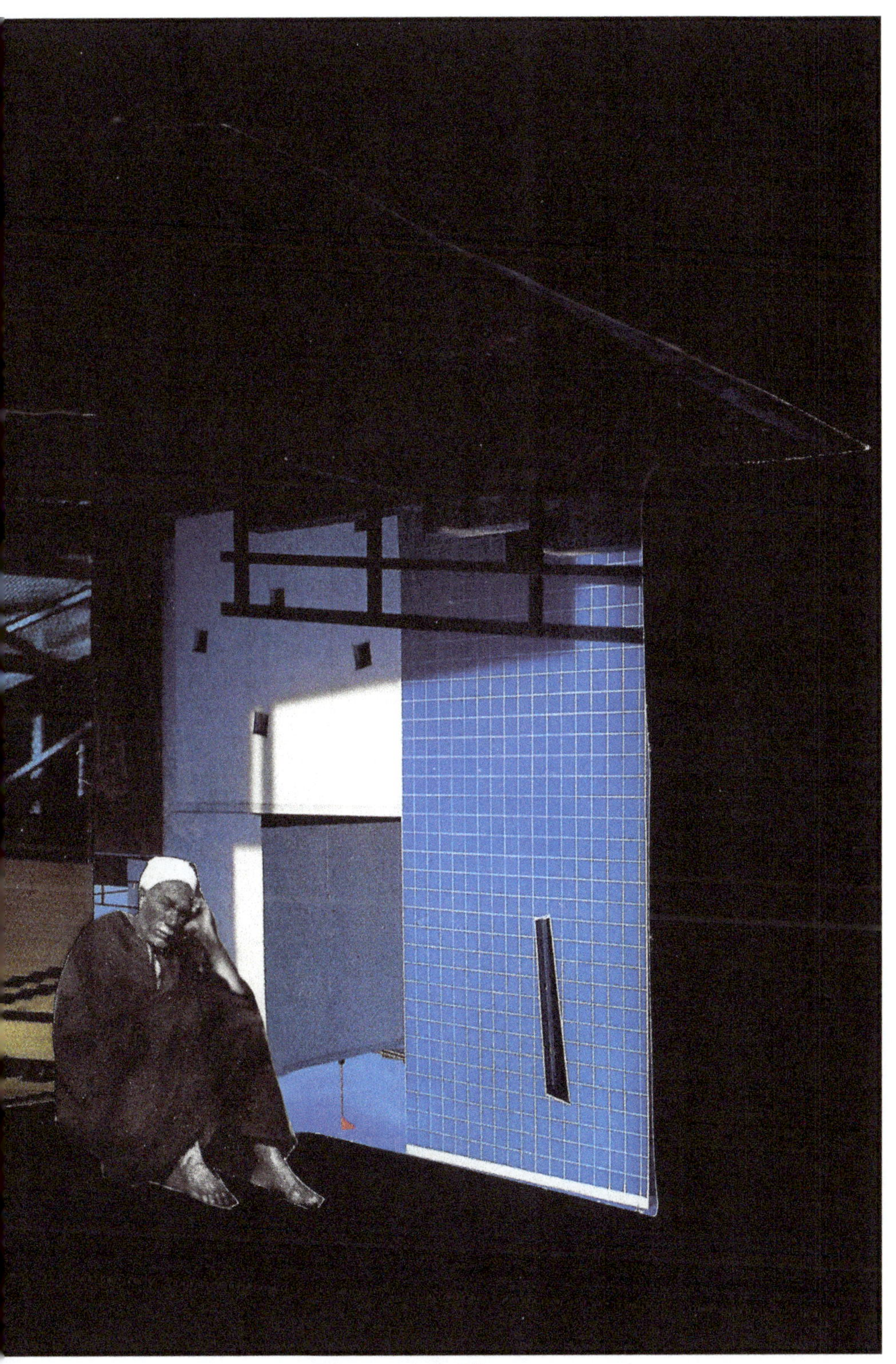

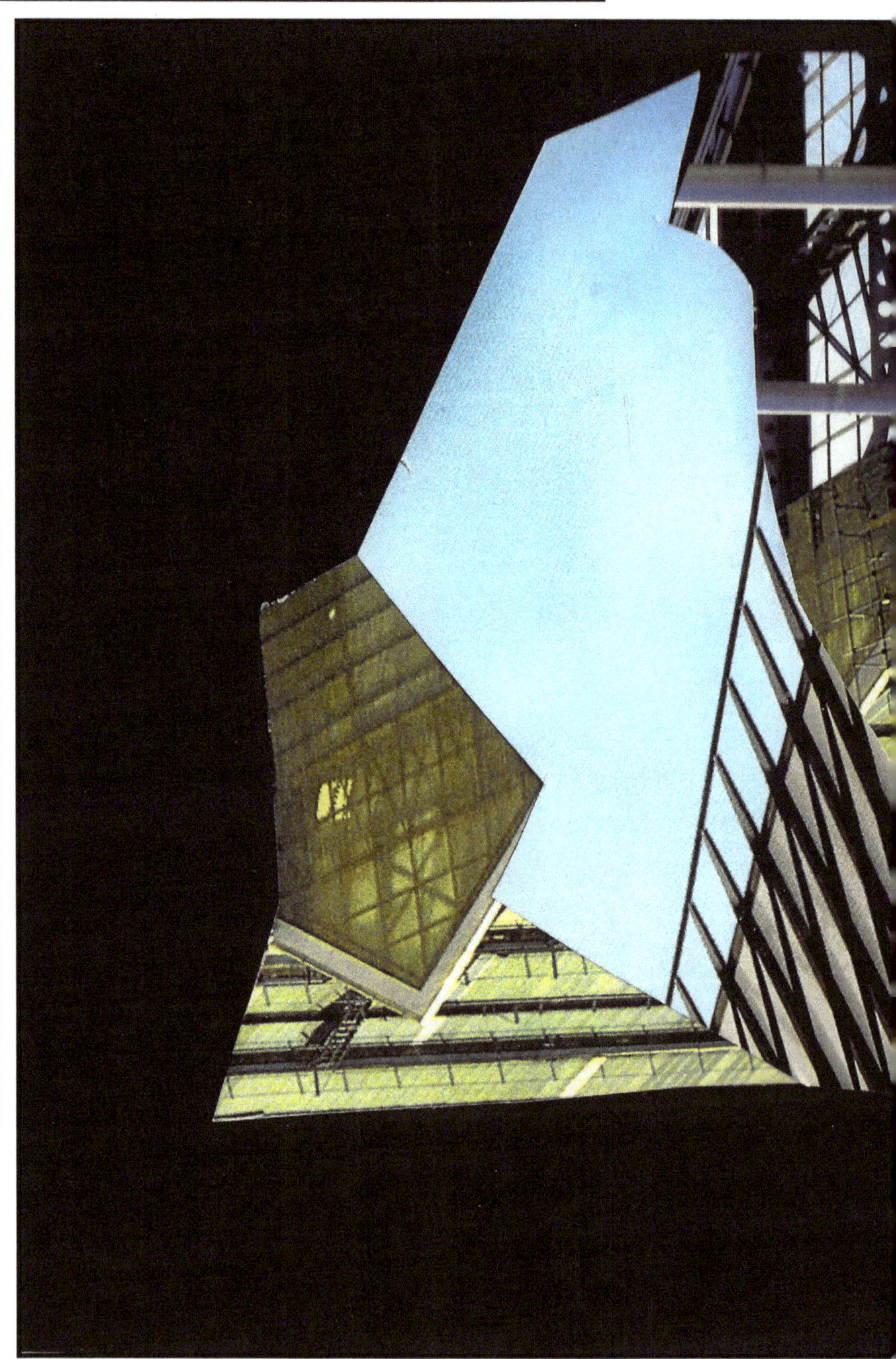

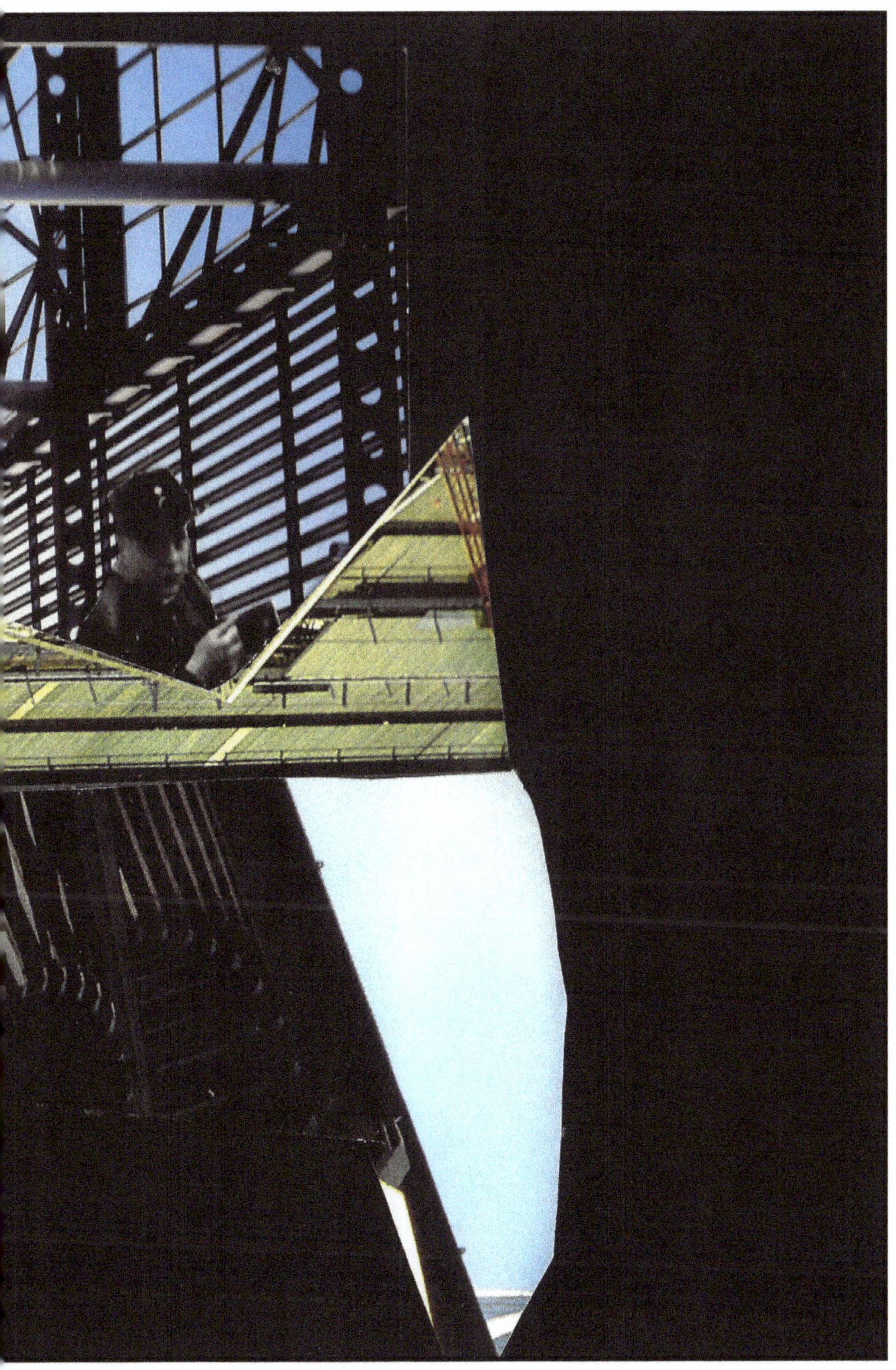

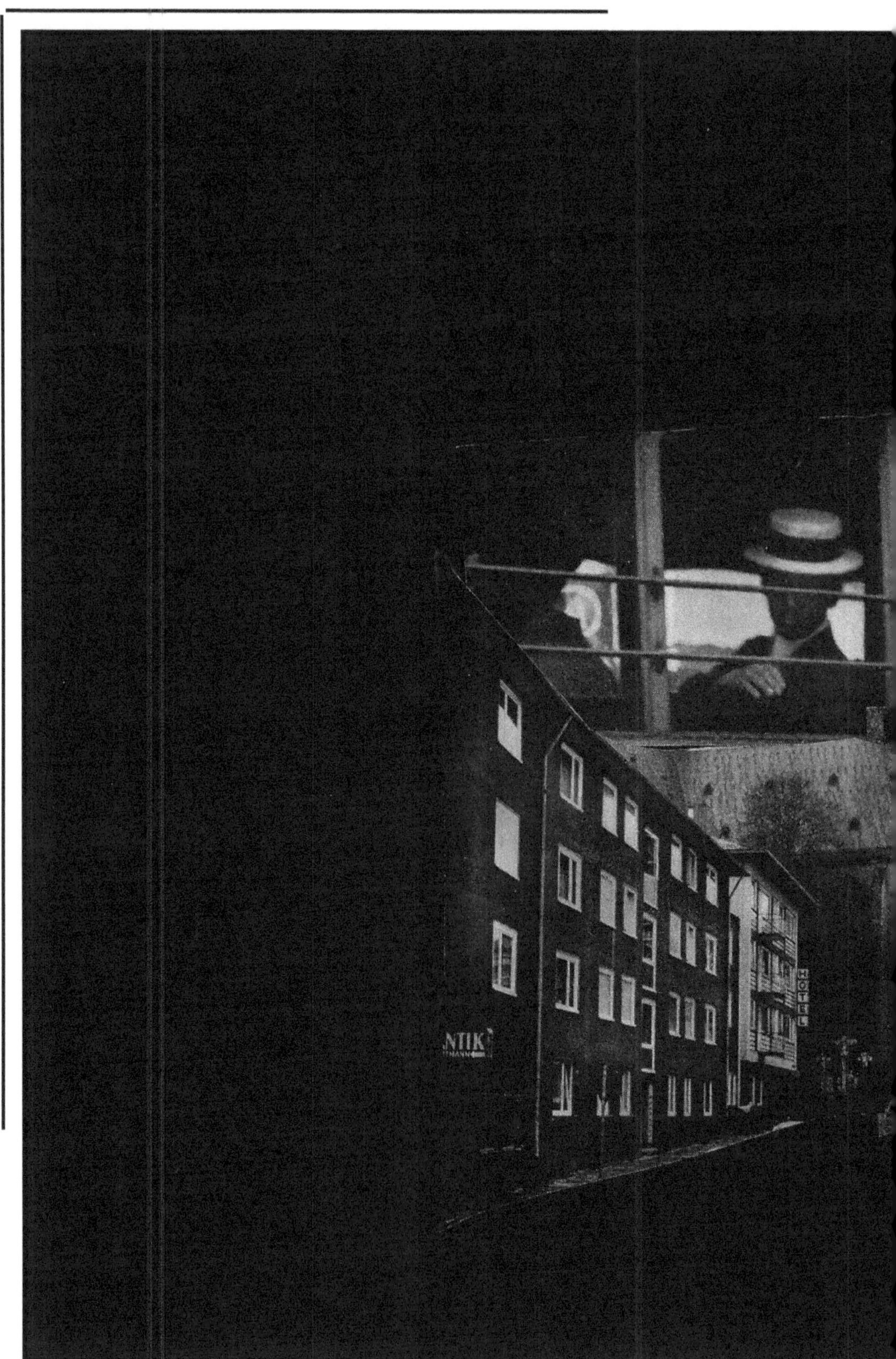

NTIK
HOTEL

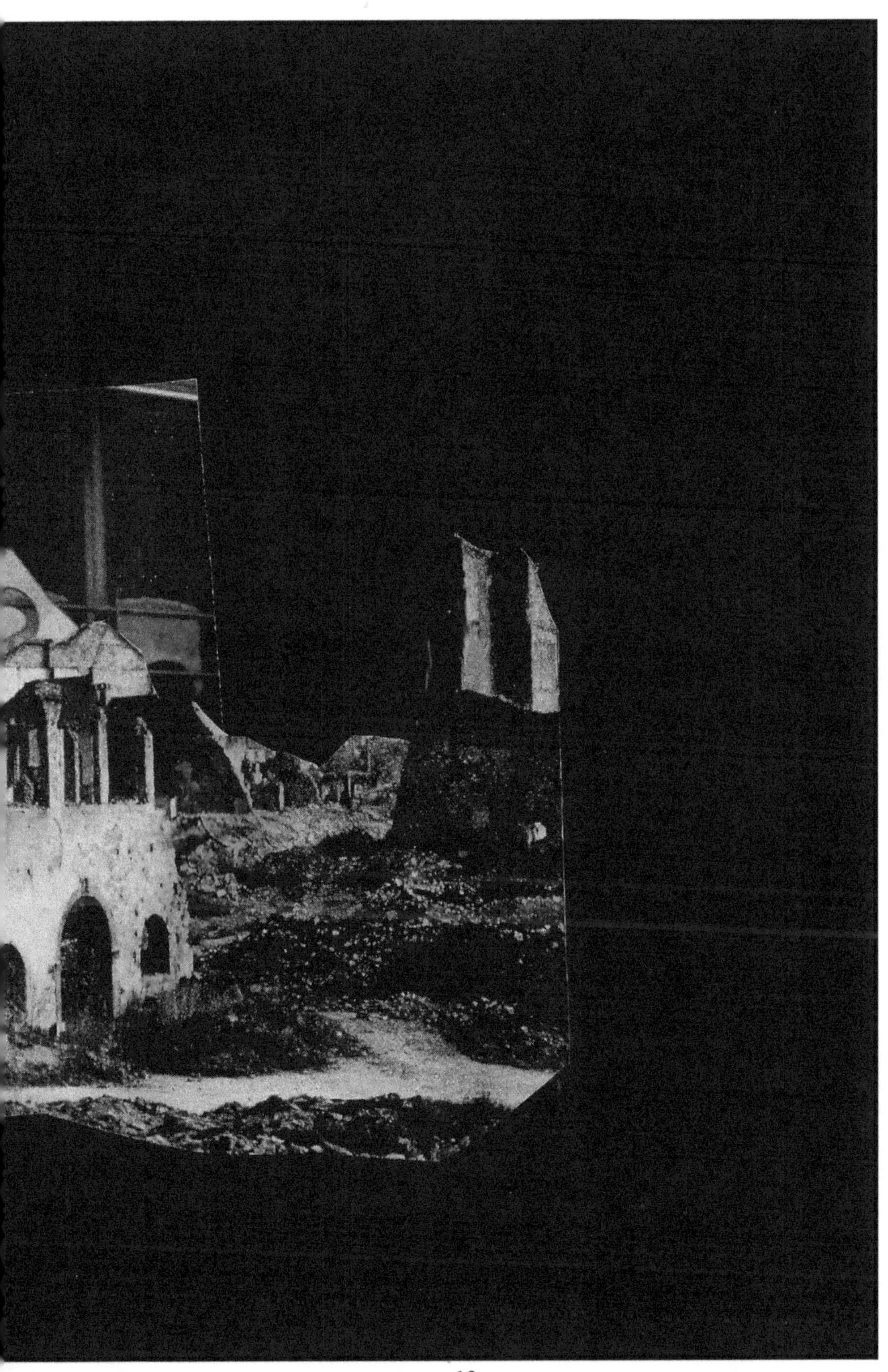

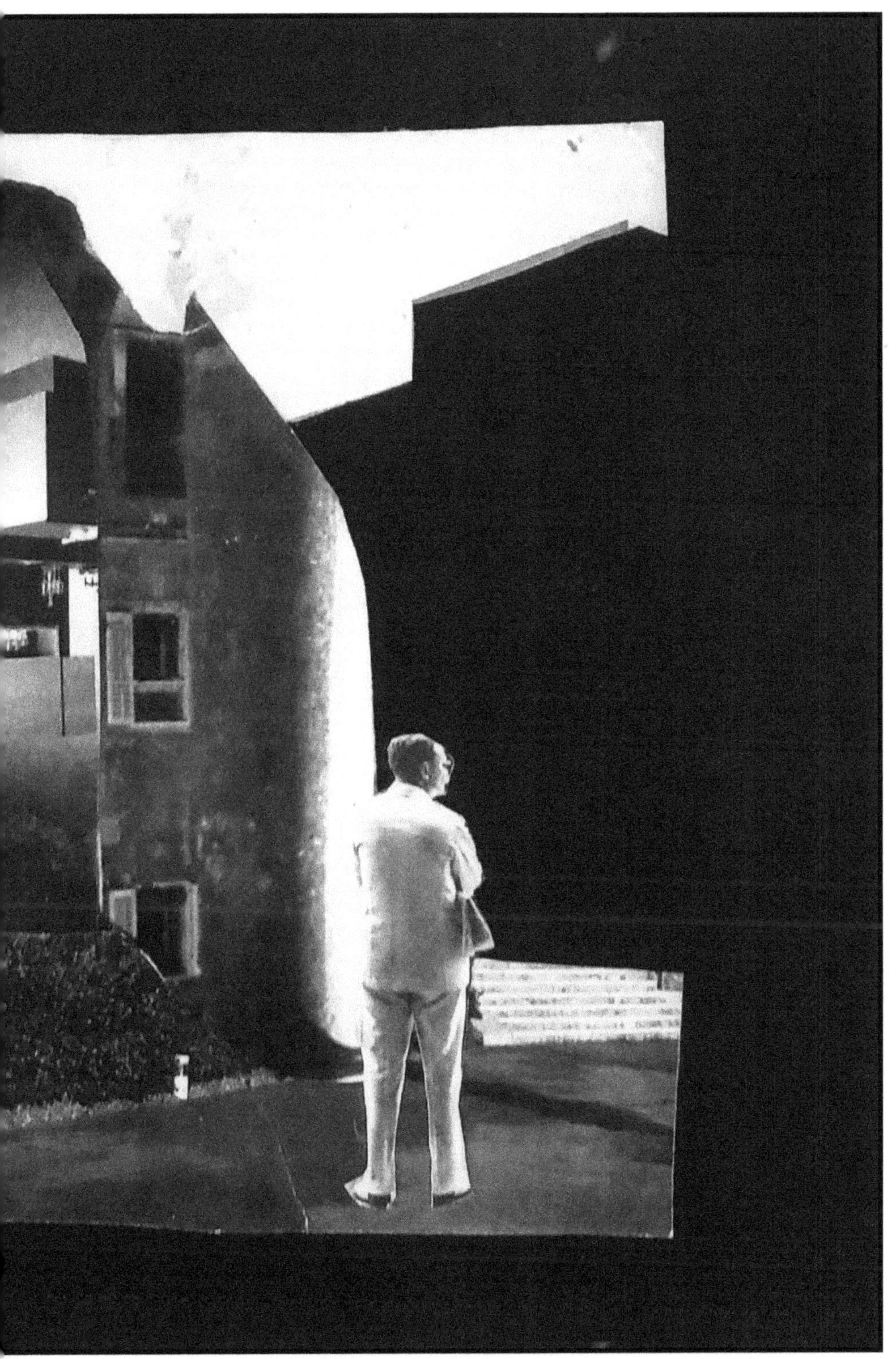

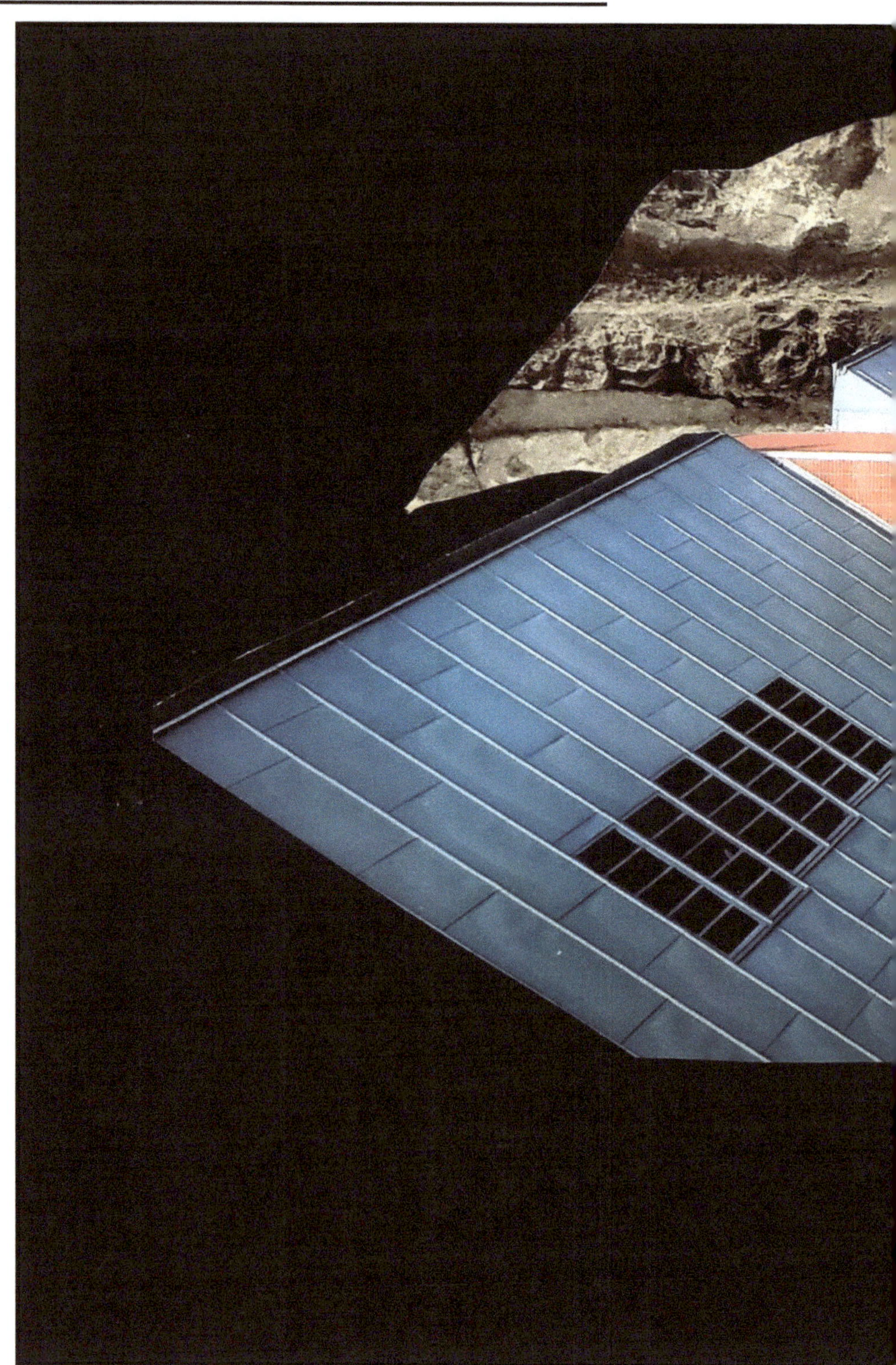

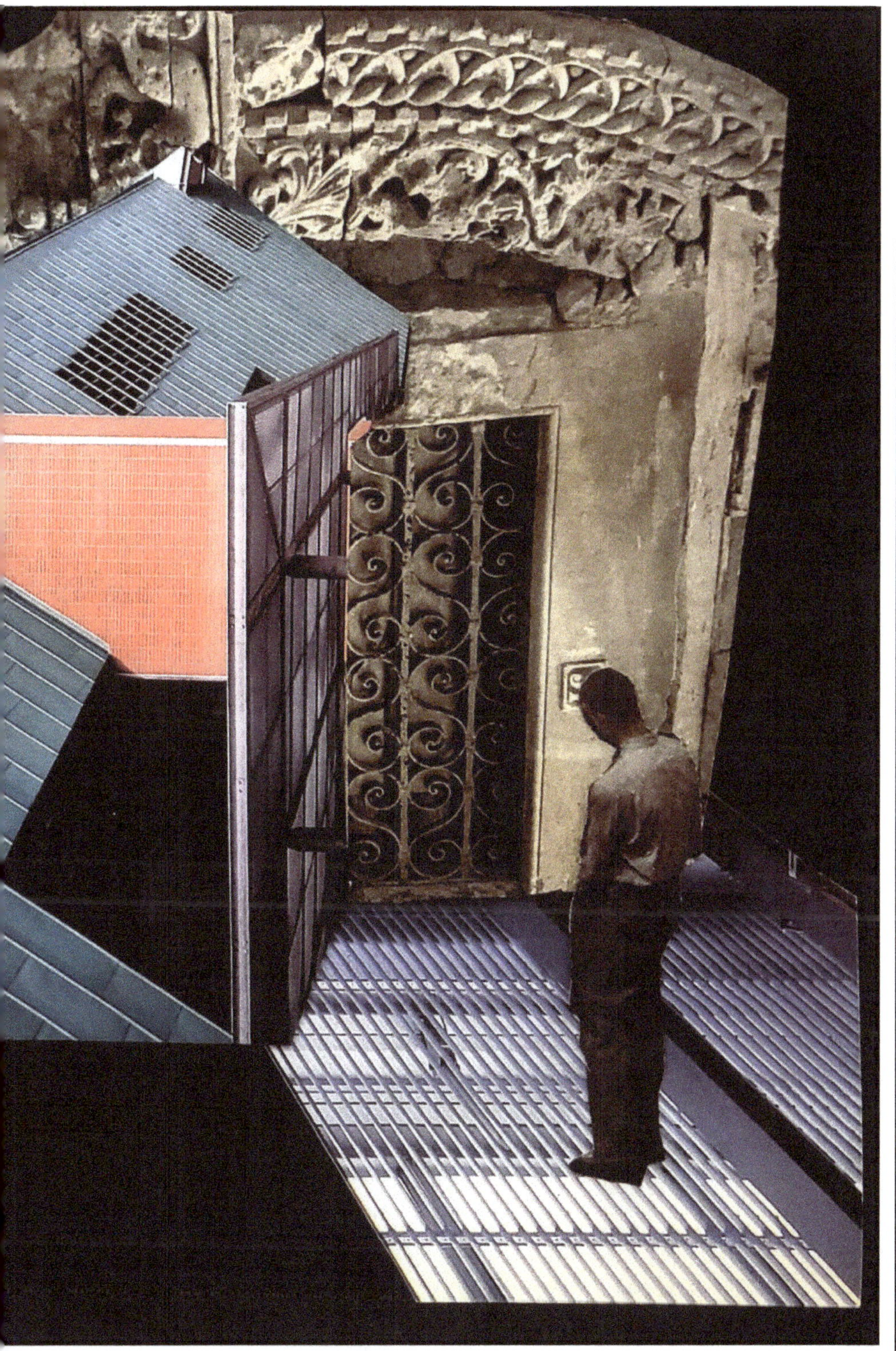

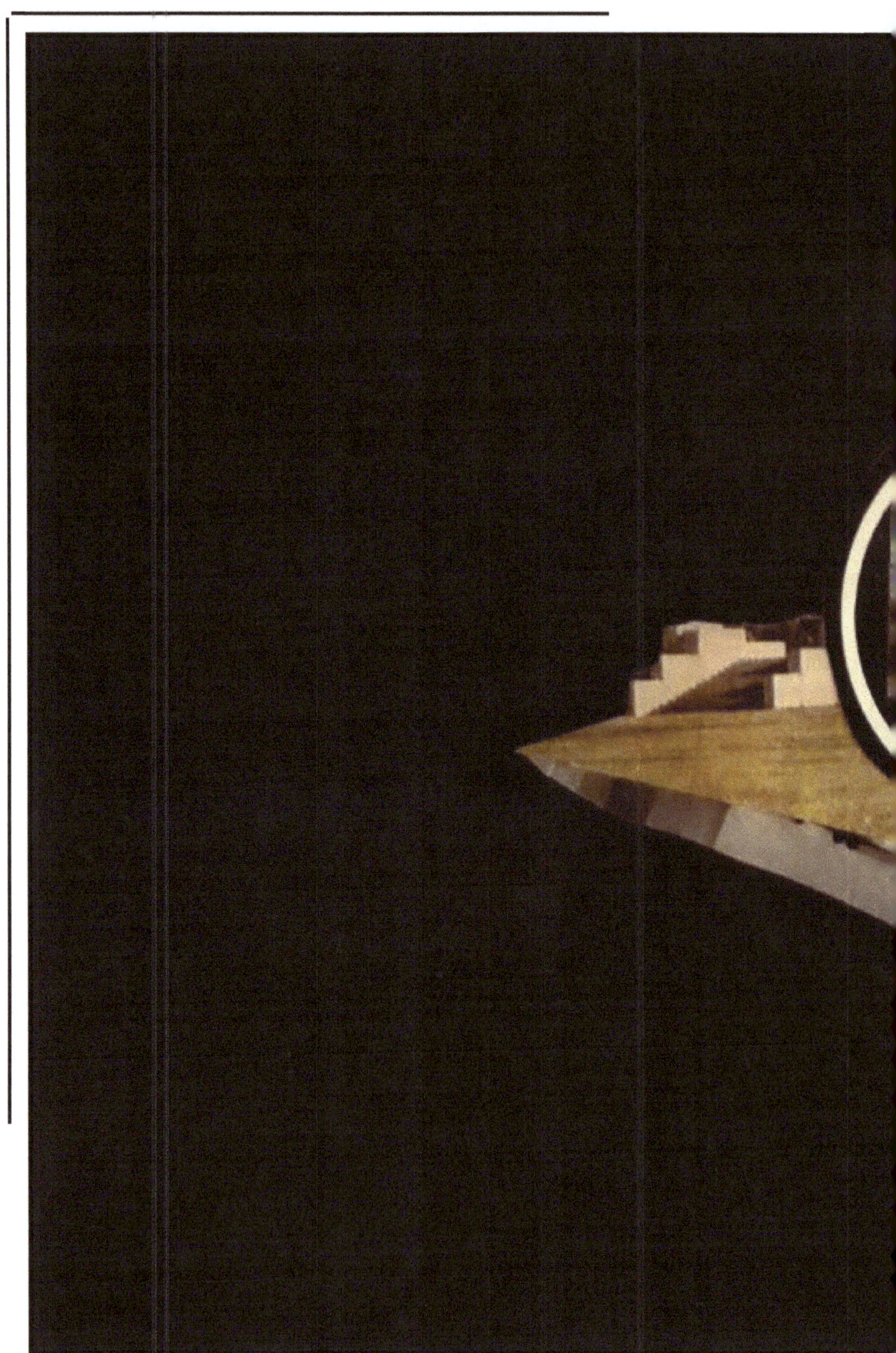

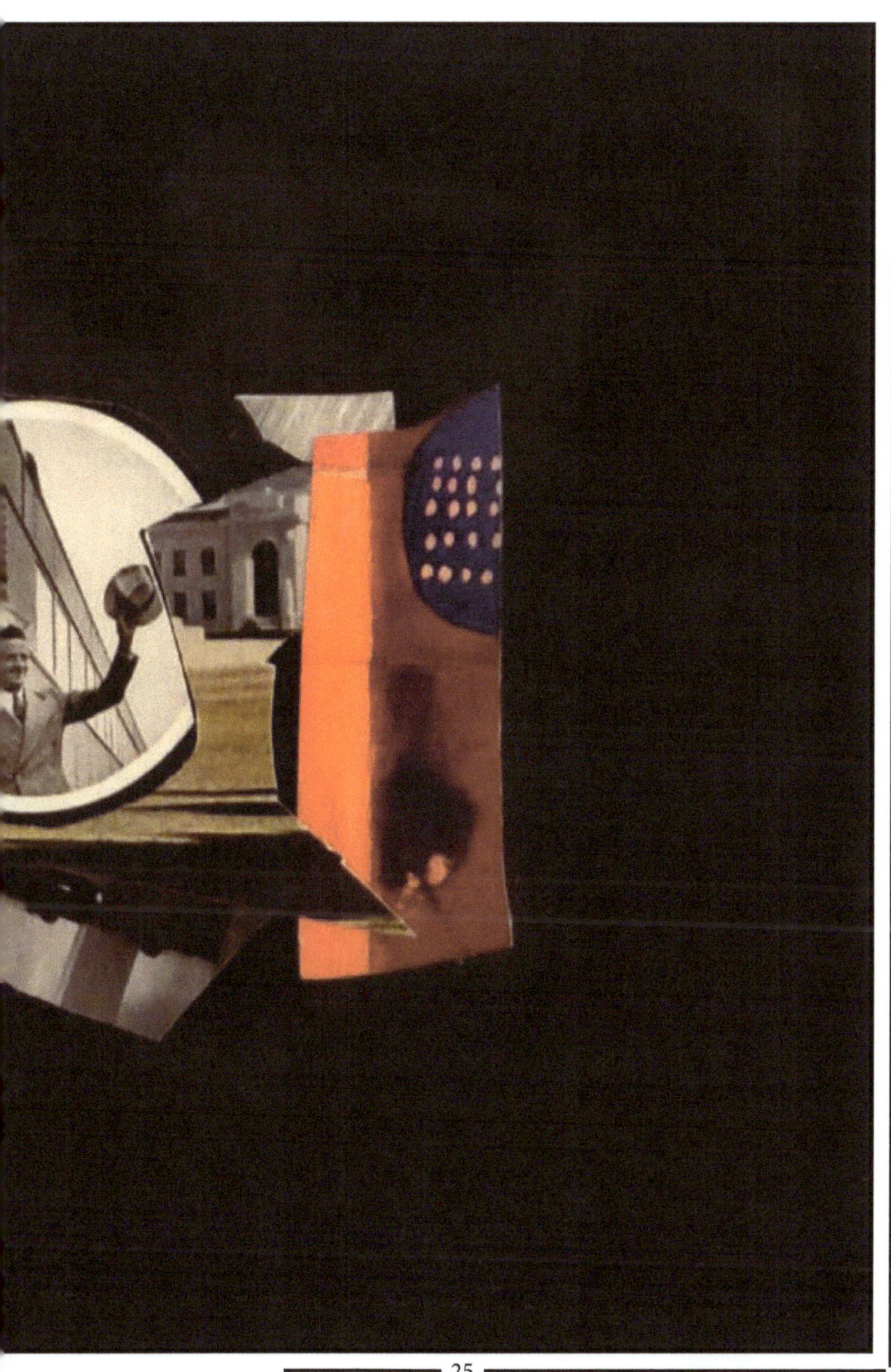

Vacuous

Leanne Hoppe

It's here but not here.
It's dull, dead leaves and forgettable tree trunks.
Patches of color with light coming through.

Look how it becomes nothing
when you forget what you had recognized
as object. Instead, forget the outline.
Forget the tree.

Look instead at the—what
it is, if not object. Pixel,
if it were a screen.

And for what's in front of me,
color? Is that more than air

And somehow not empty.

Swallow the vomit that rises to your mouth.
Call it automatic.
The sun is shining.

This isn't how it's supposed to be.
The cardinal mocks me from its perch.
What is the weight of air?

I'm counting the nothing,
the light from today's walk.
I'm thinking of nothing.
Noise in the distance.
It takes a long time.

legality of feathers

Shana Blatt

our propped bodies, still warm
with sleep, mimic cycles running
the dryer drum raw in late afternoon:
a mouth full and working.

my back to the windows;
the pane with no sash spits reflections
and rot-worthy light. i thought we
were flowers pending.

we render each other bloodless.
the walls strain to hear in our voice
an echo of humanity, flayed and bleating.
there are skins bearing our resemblance

in the marble of a temple's floor.
the tree blisters over the sapsuckers;
and we transpose their drumming
just behind our ears, or in return

envelopes empty of tongue.
en route (indefinite), we fasten phantoms:
ducks who would touch down dead upon
the river rattling through the meadowlands.

we slip past the still-watered docks tetherless
even to the moss binding its boards below,
i watch, floating, from the window,

body unmade in the circular ferocity of time.
the smell of maple at the back of my
hissing throat kicks the cranberry
extract further from my heart's rough.

on someone's frothing bedroom
floor, i leave a lucky self to thaw,
her winter plumage drained
of color, blood feathers
writhing in their sheaths.

in the stretch of smoke, we

make homes out of intentions.
the birds who fly over us on
their way to roost pull me

toward them by kite string—
i am the child of balloons,
cursed to the terrestrial.

Submerged

Birdee

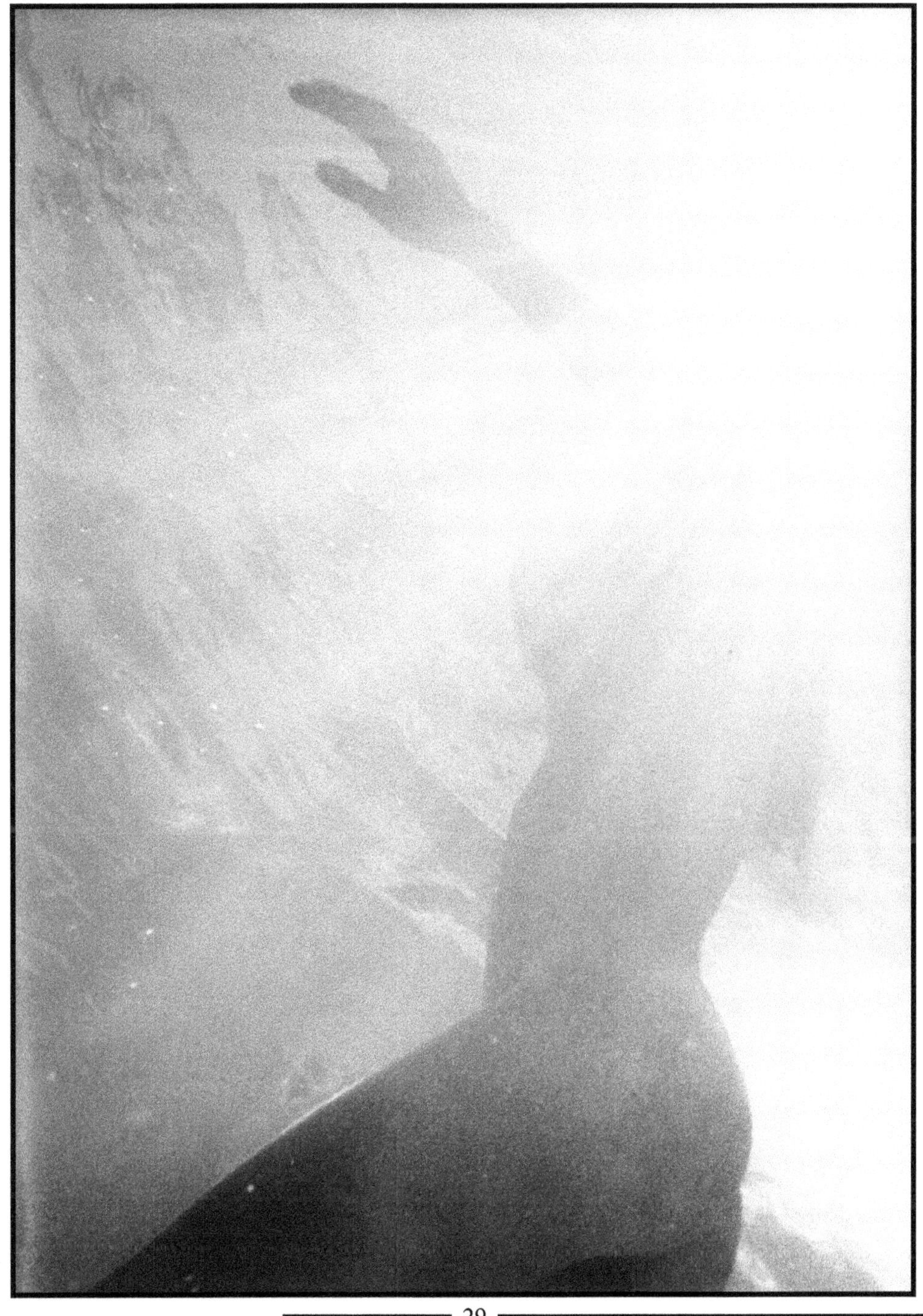

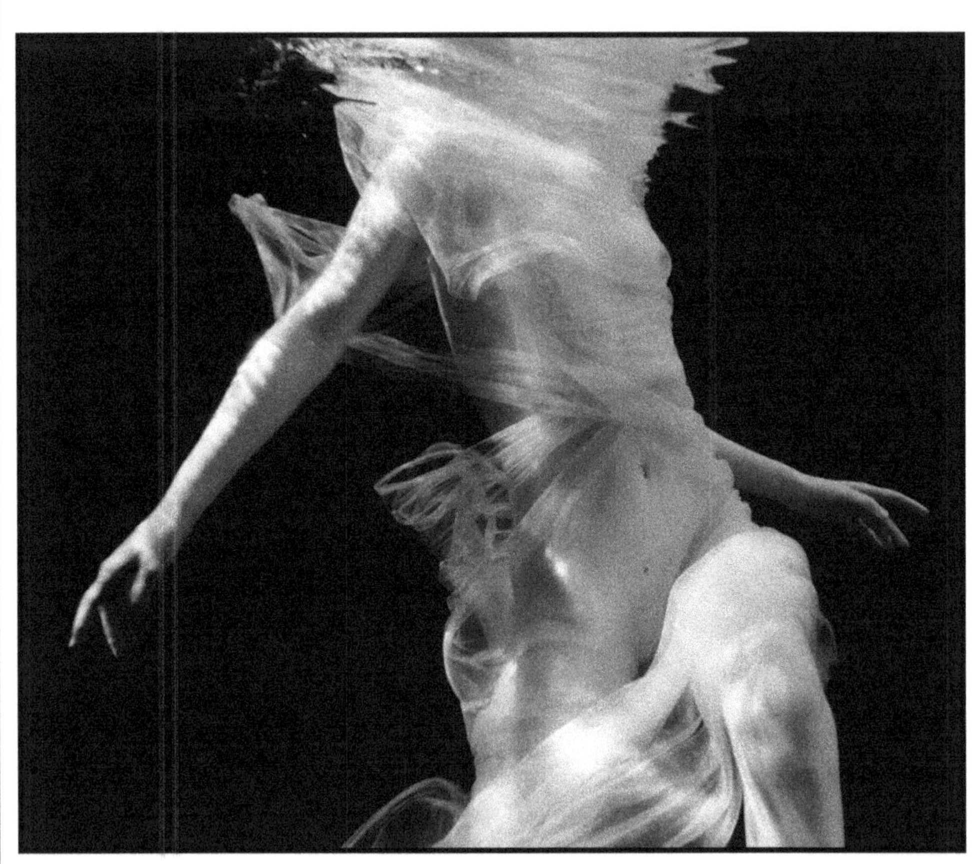

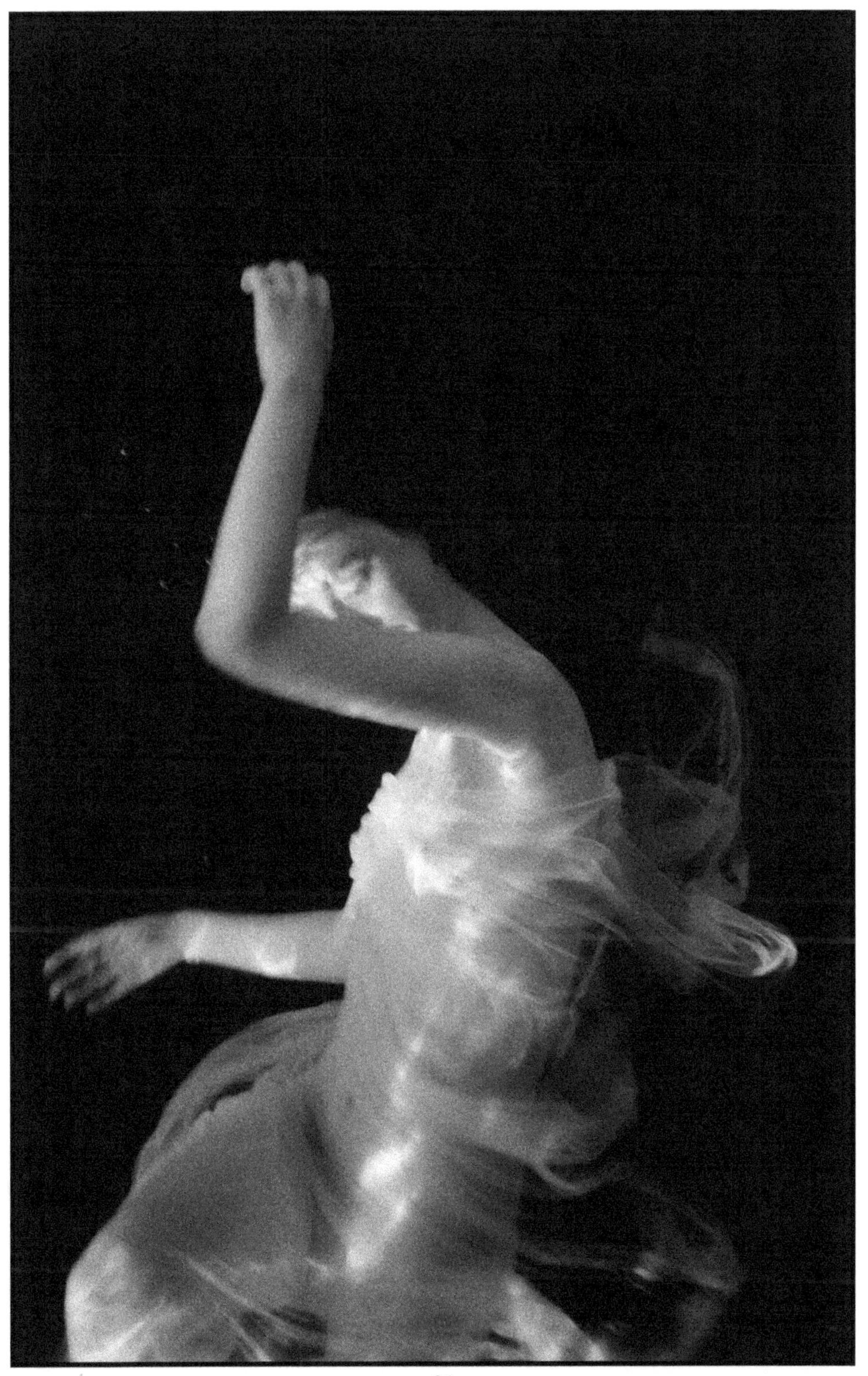

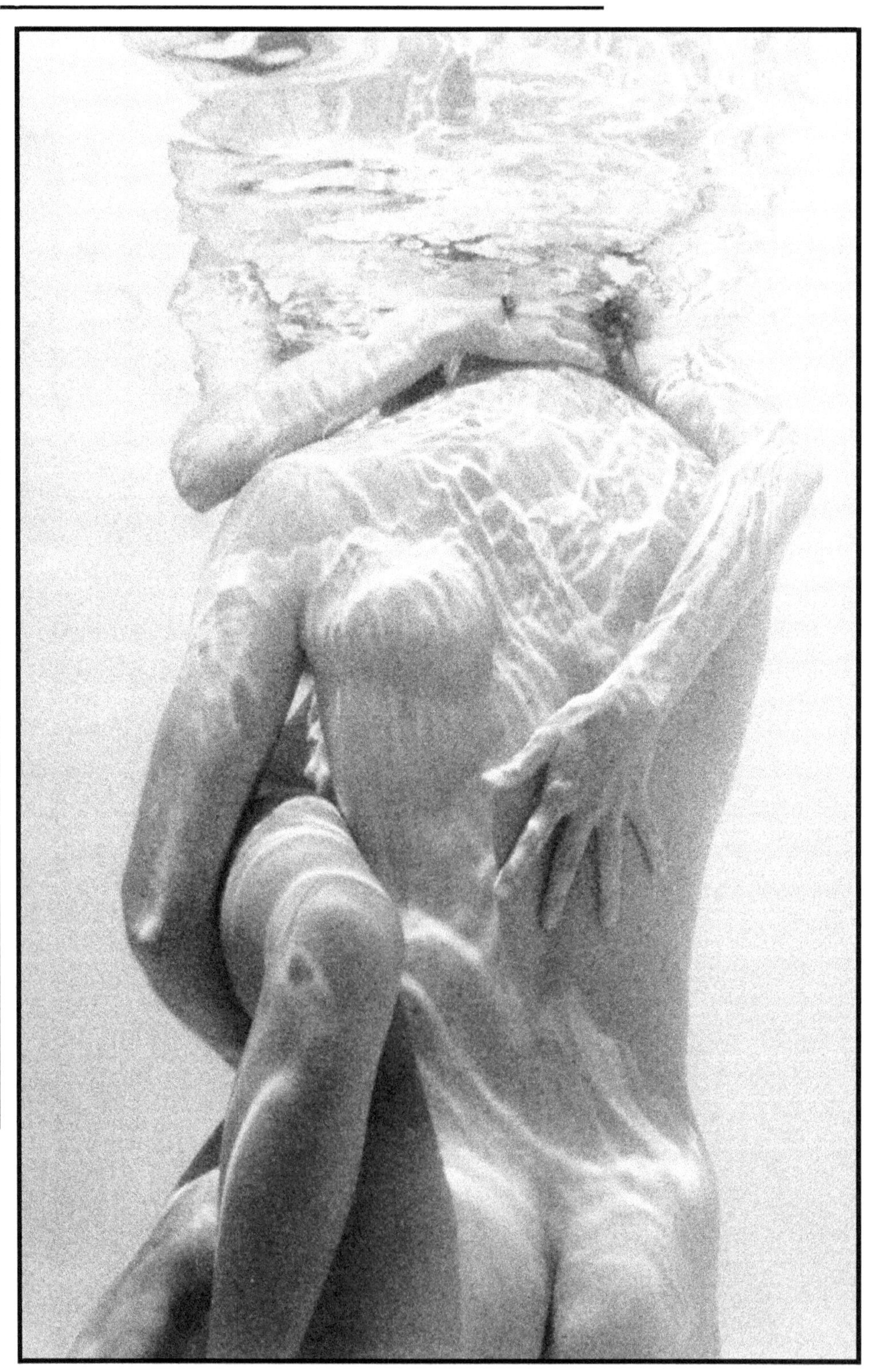

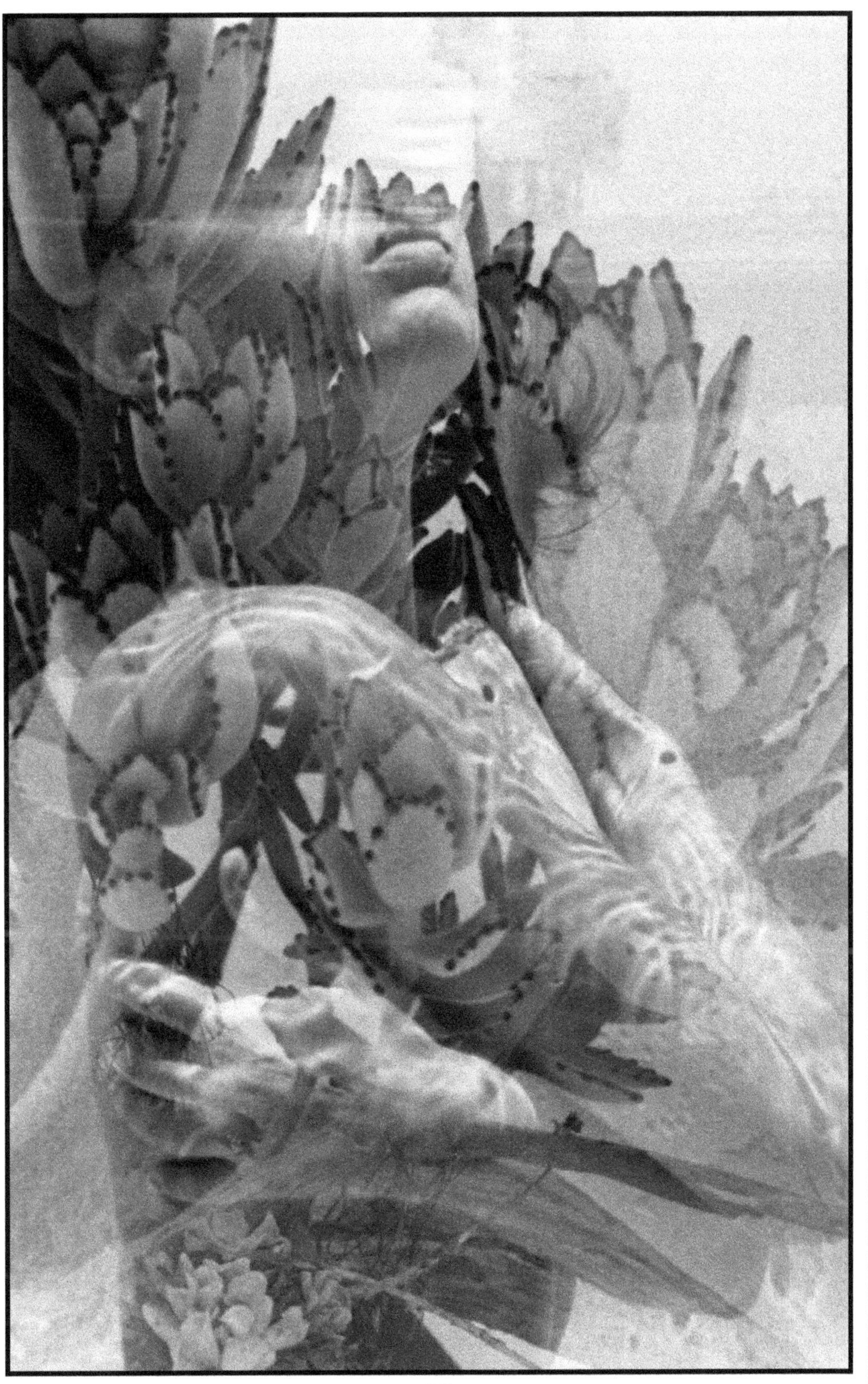

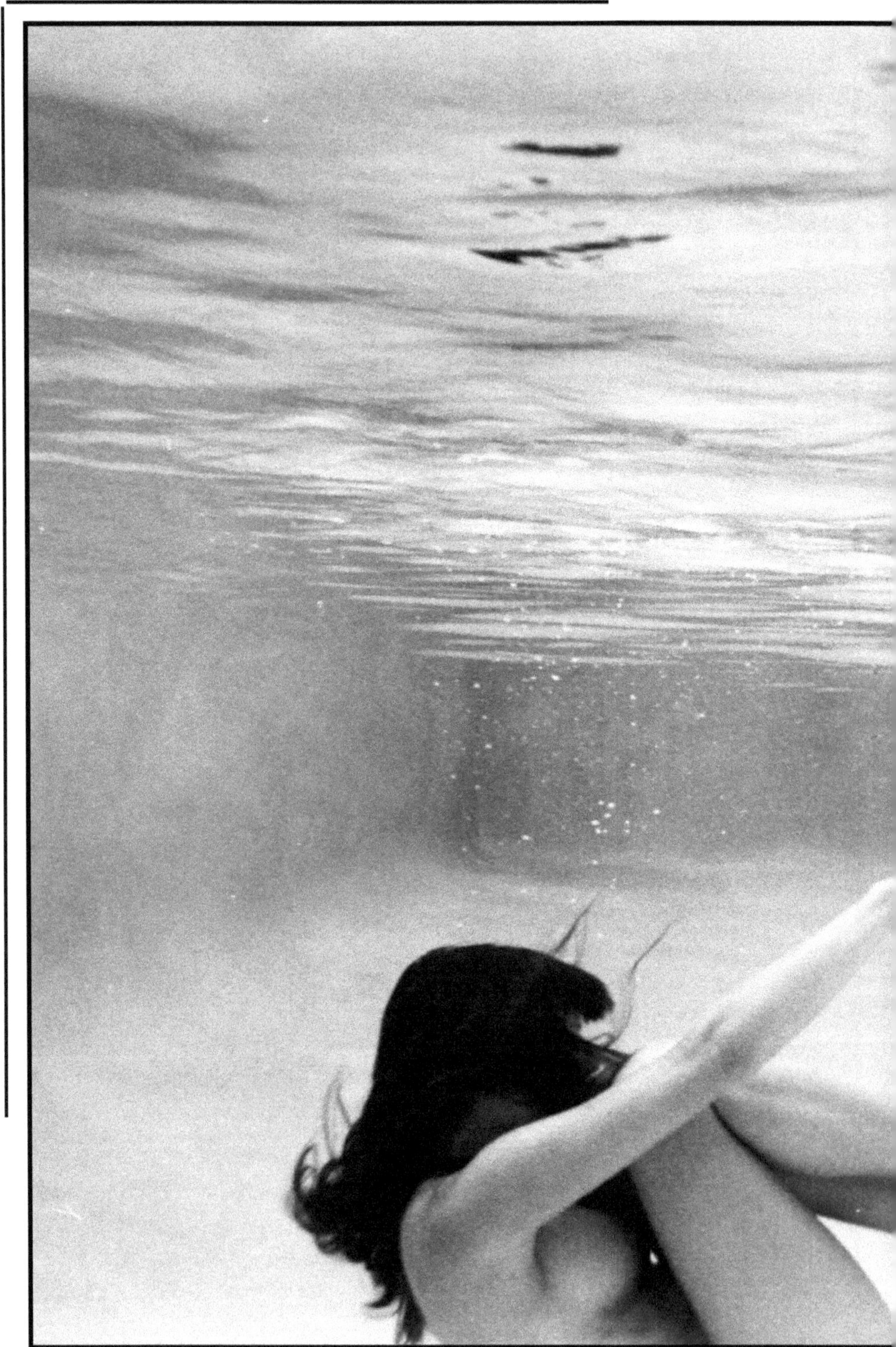

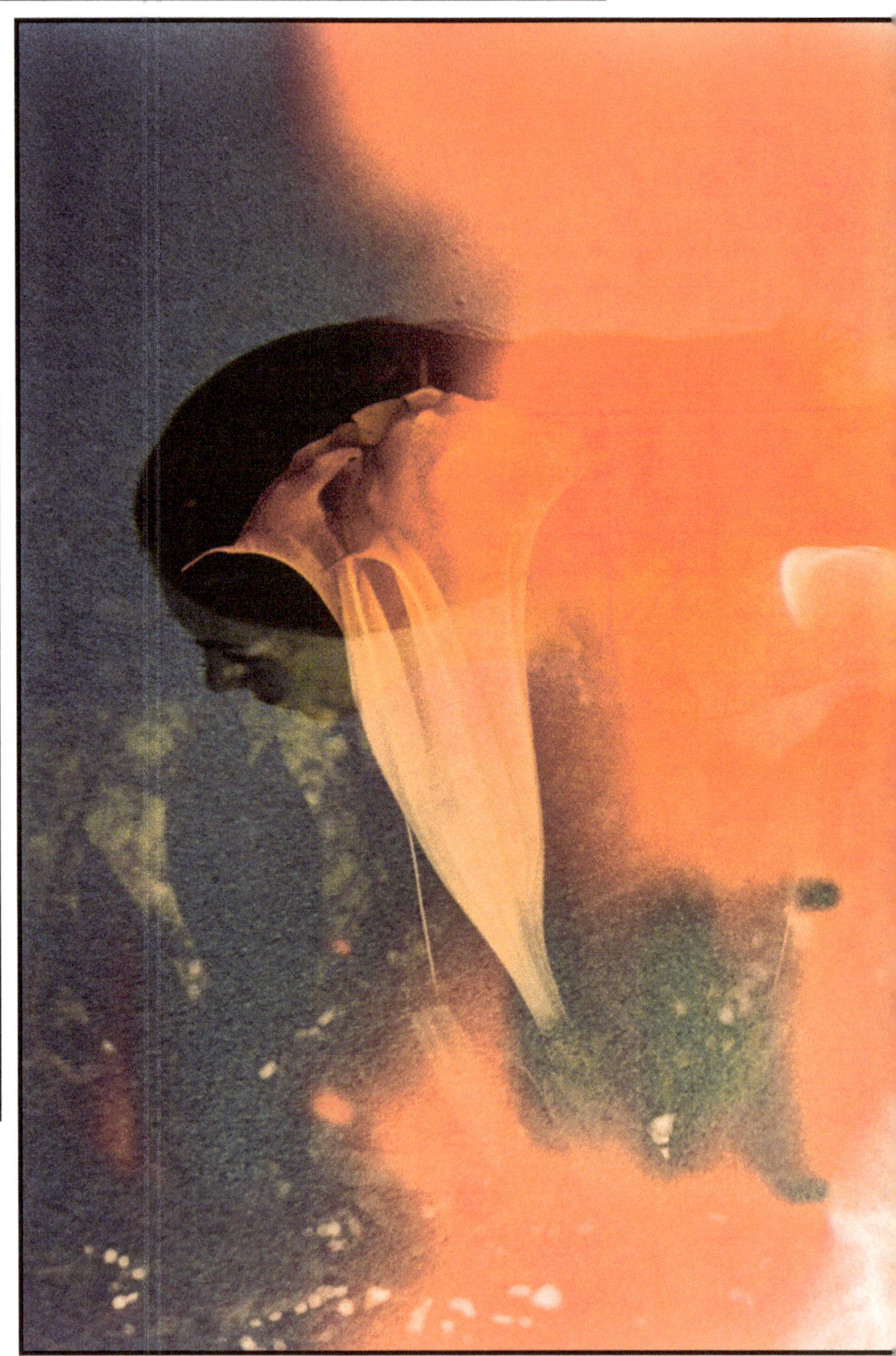

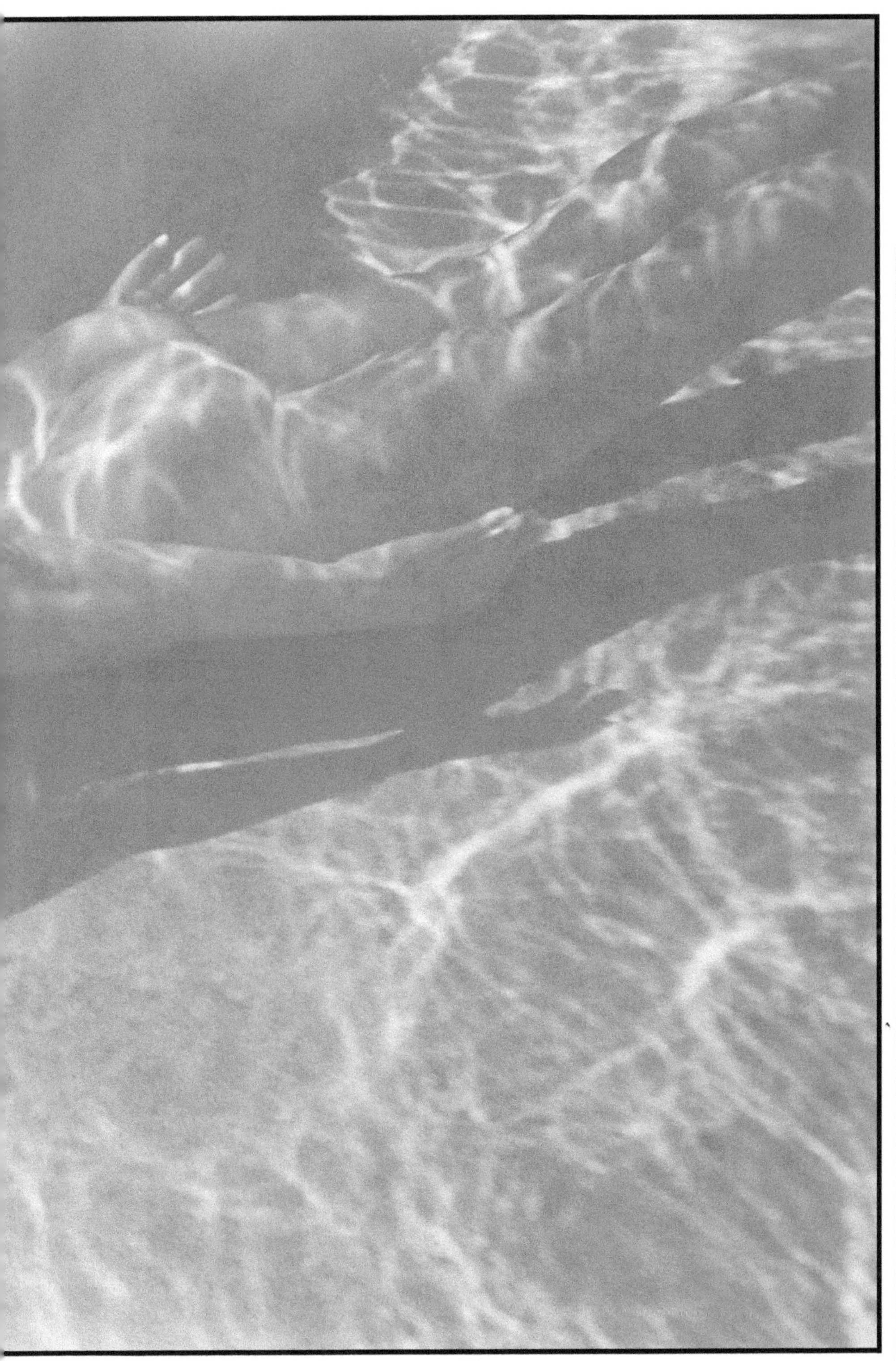

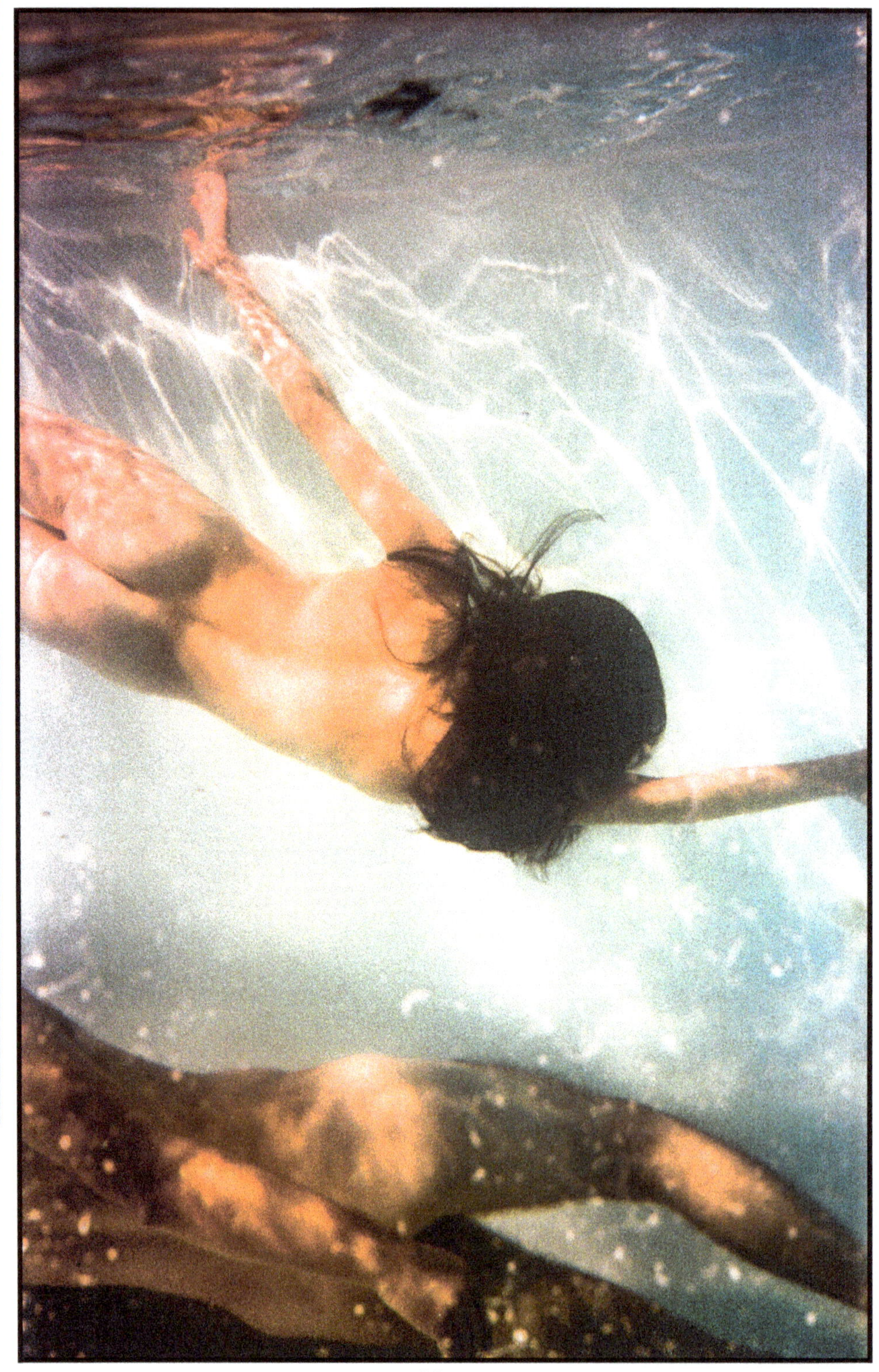

Virginia

Amanda Shaw

I wonder if you remember
Up there   in the Appalachians   watching hawks
Rust tailed tethered kites

        Taunting gravity

Wingtips skimming the wheat field below
Remember how it used to be before   something
A gear in the old grandfather clock

        Slipped   loose

Sending metal sprockets   reeling
Jangling

        Into forever   severed   bits

The great bird pulls up
Doubles back
Greedy eye scouring the sea of gold
While you watch
Maybe   not remembering
The haze of cue chalk   the clack of ivory
Wrapped in that brown blanket cocoon
Turntables and pencil smudged palms

Do you ever think   back

As your binoculars train on the patrolling birds
To the last time we saw you
To a day   less   addled
When the movements still spun

A head tilt   an iris narrow

A snap and dive

A screech

A whoop as the skilled pilot slices   back up
Through the sky
Claw full   of unlucky field mouse.

Playing Possum

Dave J.

I have a back door apartment.

I have a motion detector light

That doesn't see me smoking.

It saw the possum, though. &

I saw him before he saw me...

He didn't see me as any threat.

But I could tell that he saw me.

He walked past me looking up.

Pausing first.

His eyes were two black discs.

I smoked my final cigarette as

He passed me without caution.

My housemates' garbage can

Fell. I don't give a shit, really.

Plus I would not stop anybody

From eating. Not you not him.

I went to bed tonight knowing

The possum found his dinner.

Pre-Shift

Lauren Belmore

I can feed swarms of citizens
dressed nice to fatten up
for a cruel cold snap.
They do not play safe.

I can feed the man wriggling in a tattered bag
taking shelter in my doorway,
cold and confused,
asking for coffee and his mother.

(*I have not seen my friends*
for they know better)

Five years and my career has given me
certain pains:
A rotting tooth,
addictions,
a pat on the back from a friend
who has ten dollars until
next check.

But this plague,
eating the brick and mortar,
built on generations,
the young blood who thought
hardships came with the coat.
The mothers and fathers
who burnt their hands
for their children

The refuge
set ablaze
while many of us are trapped inside.

Ray said it best:
"Eating is a small good thing
at a time like this."

There is a dream but
who knows where she is hiding
now.

A Looting

Jacqueline Rosenbaum

Today, there was a looting in Locust
Valley, a classic heist. Contents un-Earthed
from dusty cardboard and concealed within
pristine, white shoeboxes which recently
housed a sexy pair of strappy black heels—
you would approve. I stole two planners from
the nineties, portfolios complete with
resumes, magazine cutouts rendered
delicate and raw to the touch. I have
your Social Security Number, pink
pamphlets from shabbat, hallmark cards signed
by your mother. At first, I thought they were
for me: *To my Beautiful Daughter*.

I stole a photo album: a trip around
the country with a man who is not my
father. Your life seemed nice: yacht parties
on Saturdays in the Summer, dinner
dates multiple days a week and love
letters signed by Mark, by Scott, by Dave, men
who can't live without you. In the margins
of October, you balance your checkbook,
and I'm relieved that you're in the green.
Spring, you run often, record your speed,
and you seem to be getting better each
week. I'm looking for mismatched handwriting
and events crossed out with a feverish
motion. I'm looking for parking tickets
and pink dreams of baby girls wrapped in white.

I study the photos of you, yellow
and orange from the years. I hold them up
and listen for something like thunder, search
for lightning, but you're barefoot on the beach
and you are the sun. It's a game, you flash
a model's smile rehearsed to perfection.
Does the man behind the camera understand?
In March, you write to Steve on sticky notes
that it's too late, you loved him once but
that was many years ago, and I relish
this reflection, knowing I'm only

a year or two away. I find your transcript
from community college. In '81
you were failing F&E Business and
The elements of Econ. You withdrew
from Retail Principles, a "Slimnastics" course.
Your GPA is a measly 1.5,
and the future is grim, academically.
I crave the others: documents tracing
Your path from '81 to '94.
According to this, the small credit you
received came from a B+ in freshman comp—
something I hadn't known I was searching for.

Blueish

Doug Dabbs

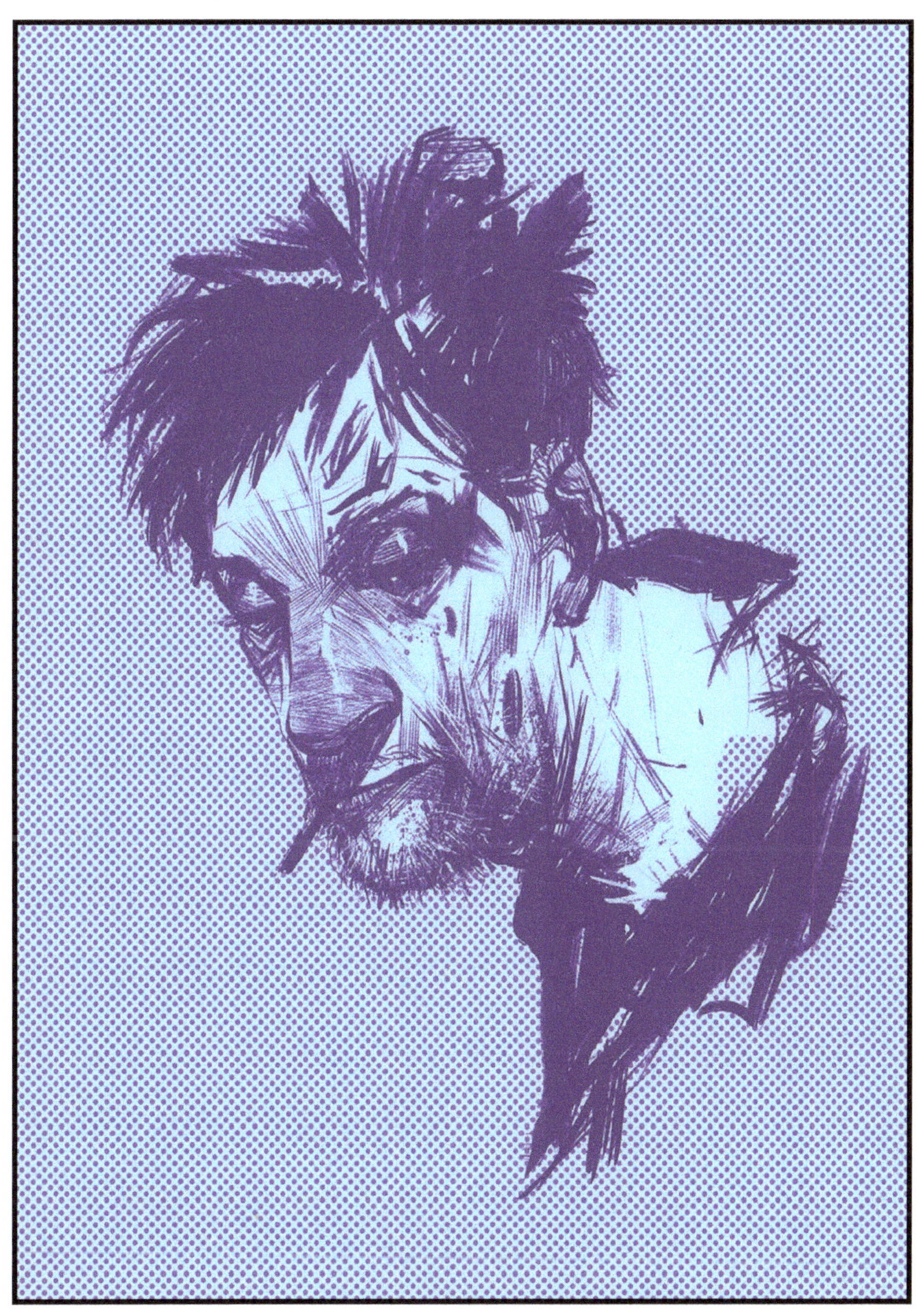

JULY

Susan DiPronio

Let's meet in August she says
how quickly she gives away July

so confident that many are still
coming, another year and another.
A book with pages yet to turn.

For me,
this one lingers precariously
each day the same as another
I pause within the quilt of time.

For her,
confident in the appearance of another July,
the present is expendable.

I, grab the light of day and the soft dark of night
and cling to,walk slowly into,examine every minute,of this July.

For life sends invisible snipers
a red dot traces
hesitates
its landing unpredictable.

KJ Williams

KJ Williams

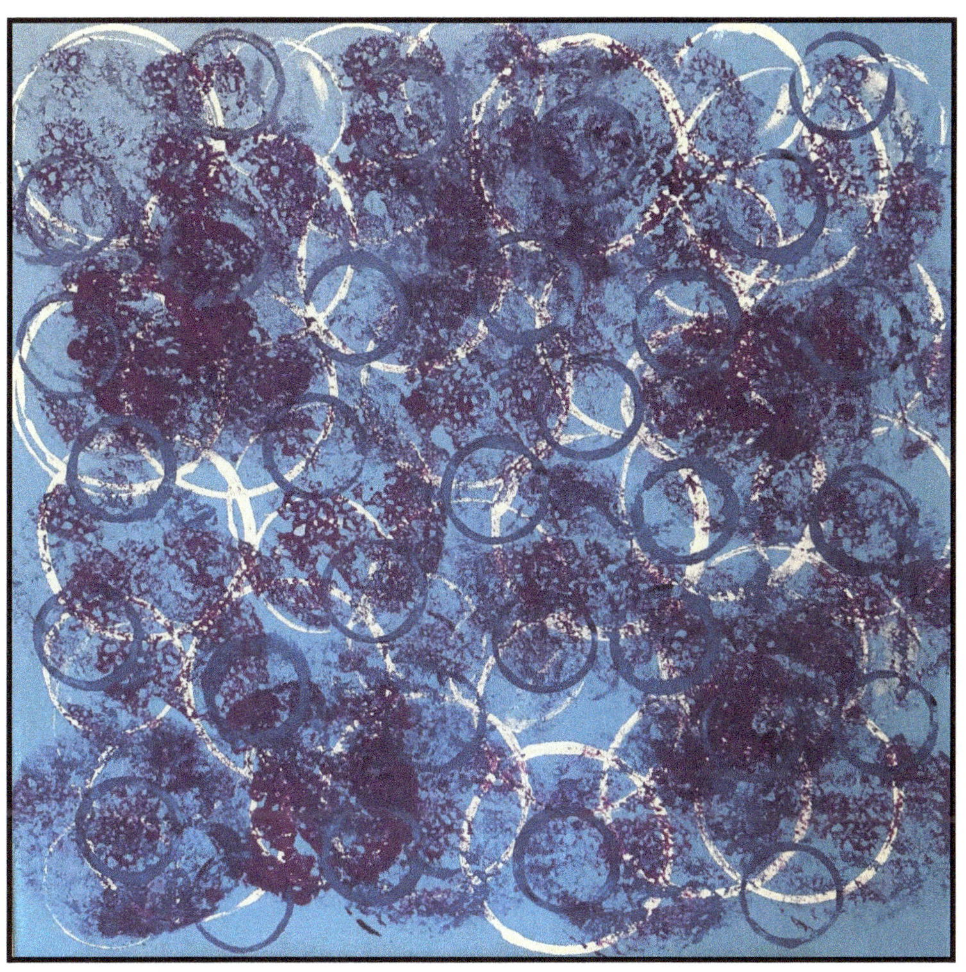

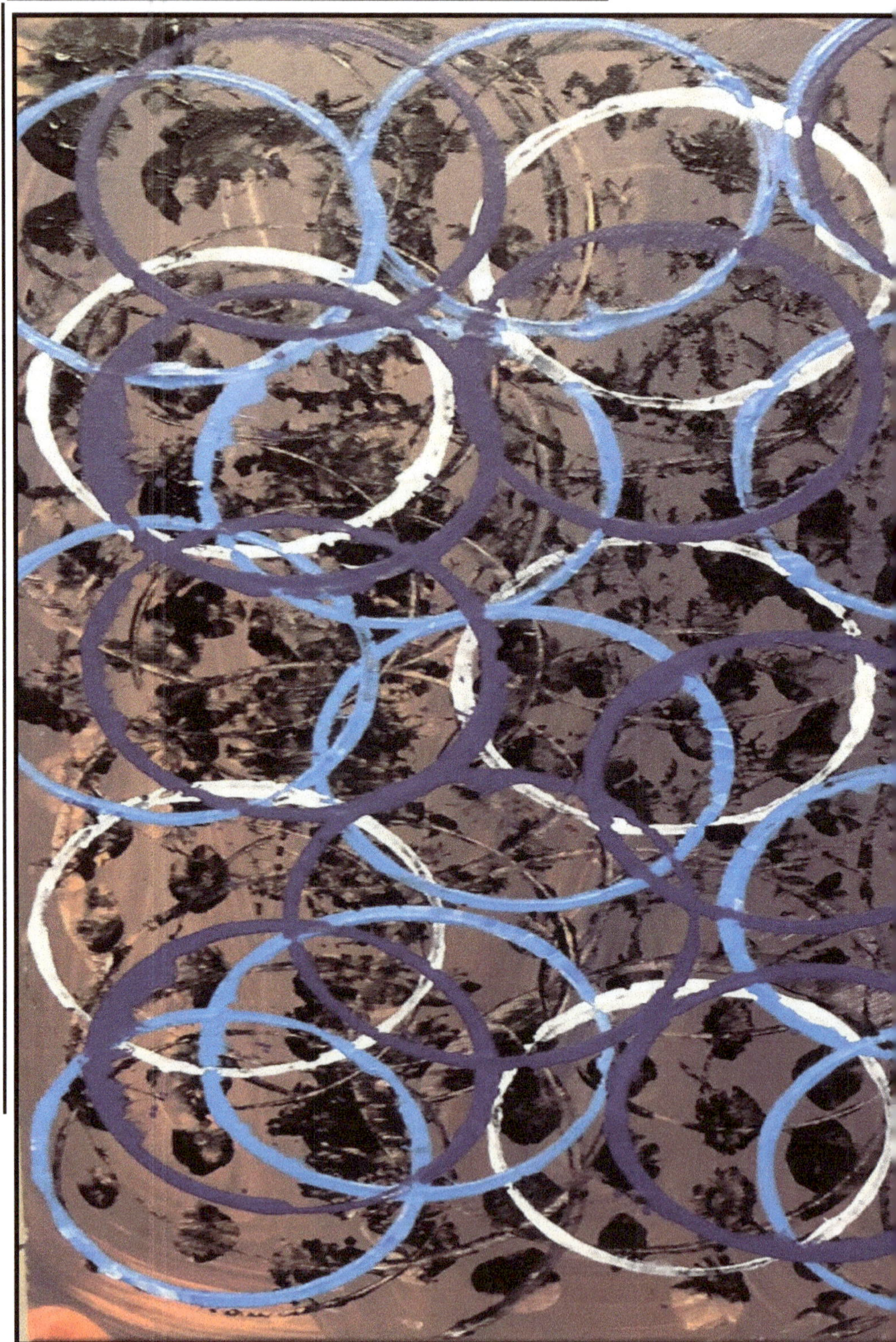

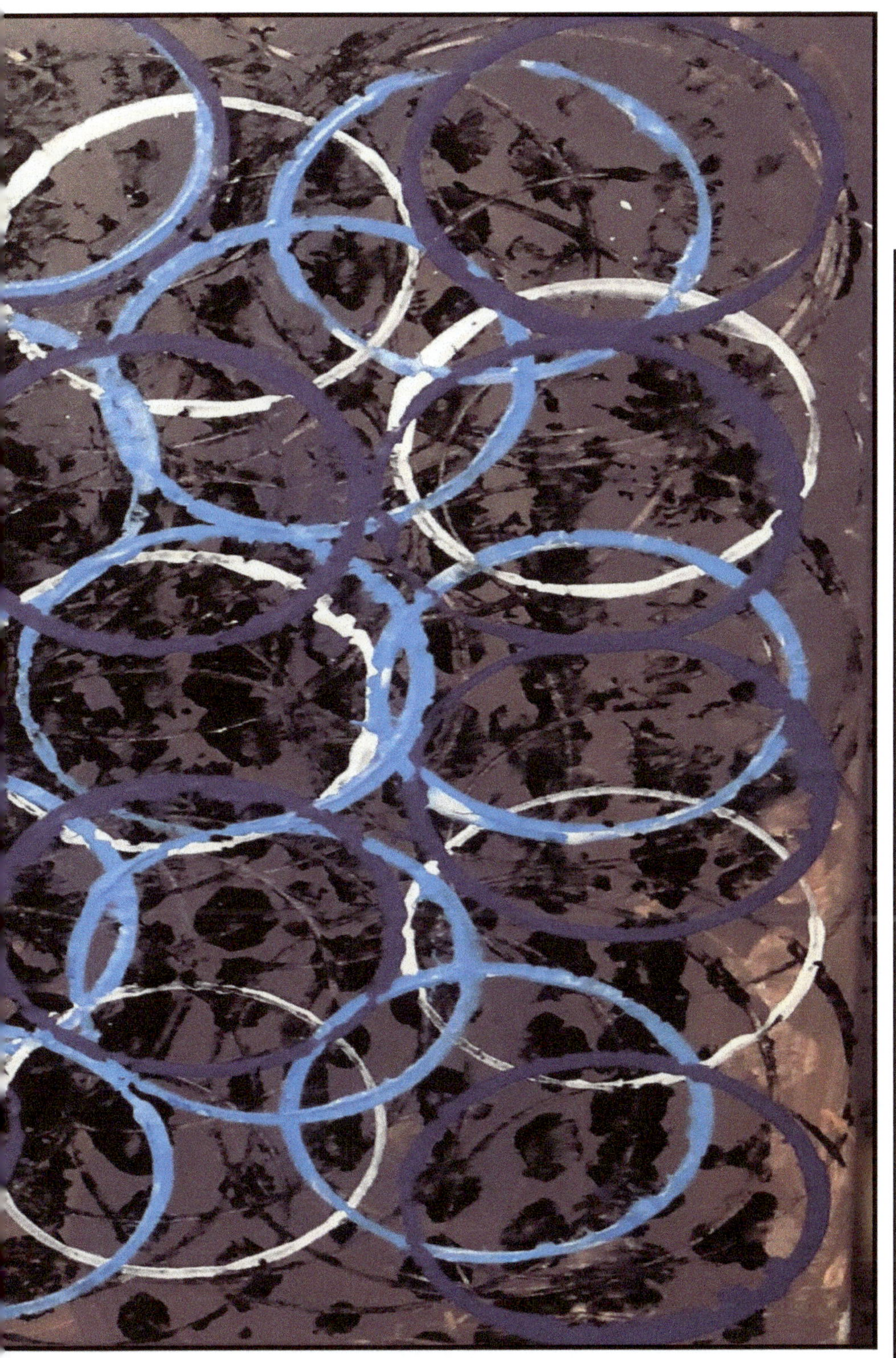

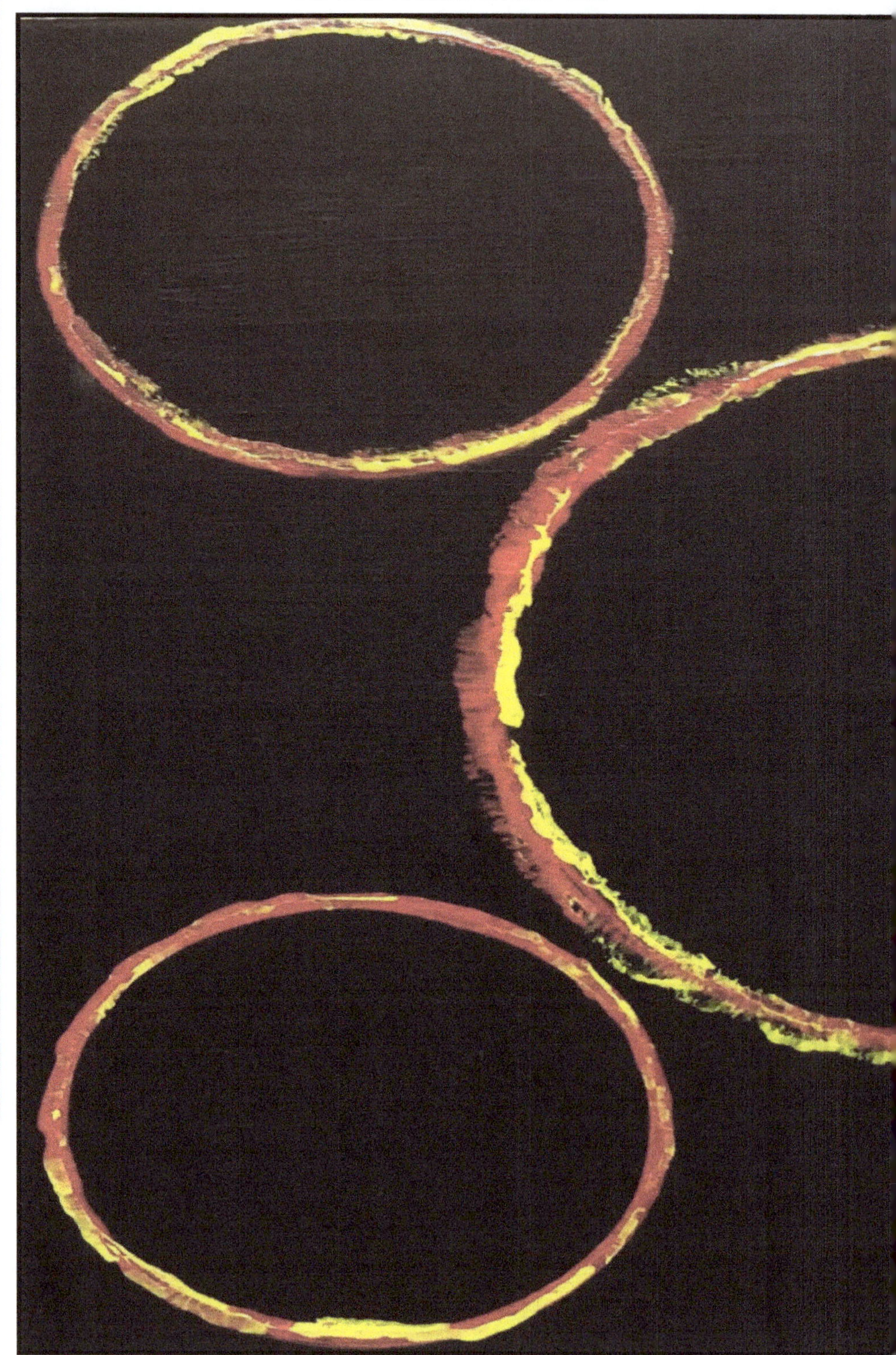

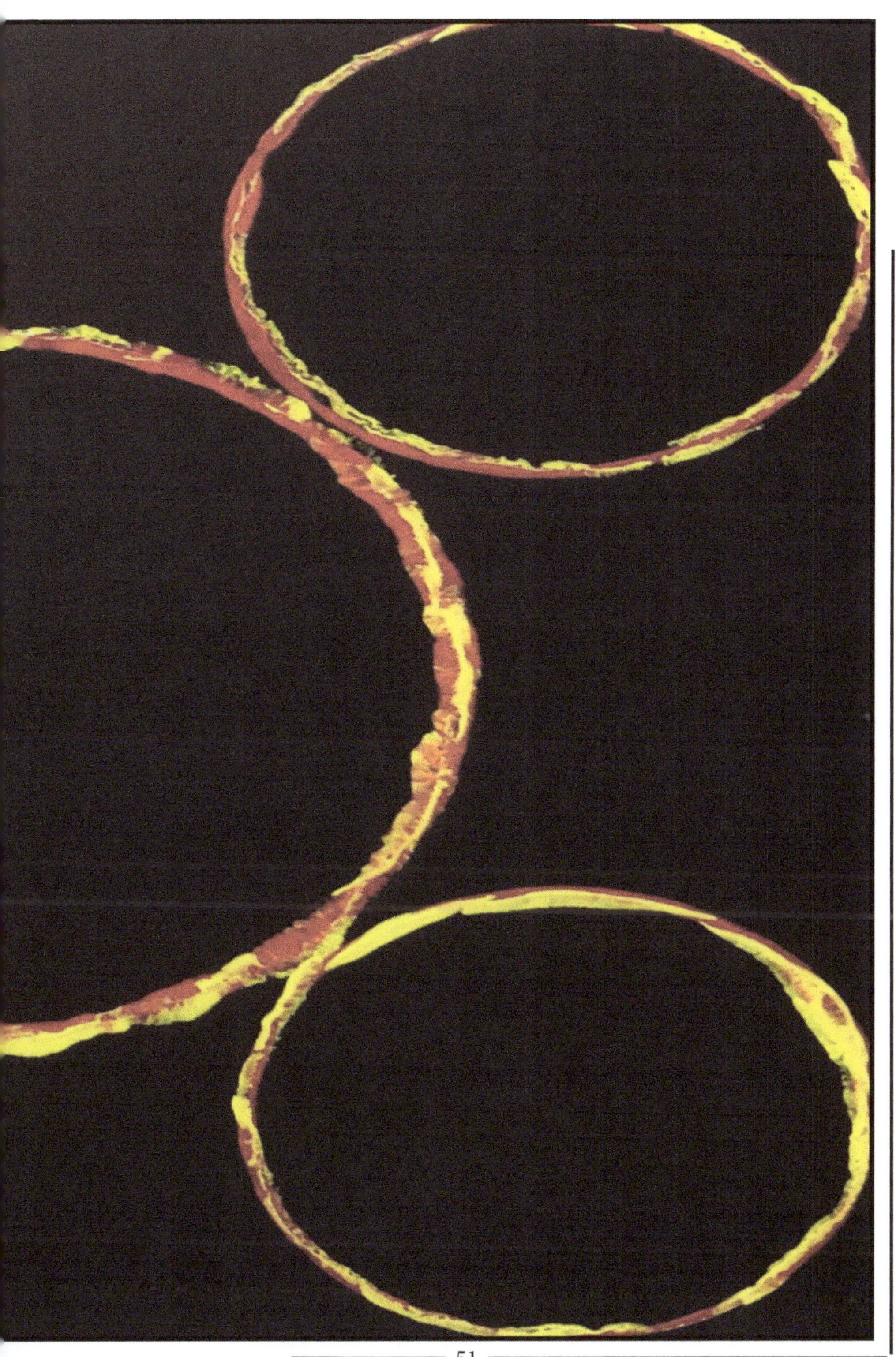

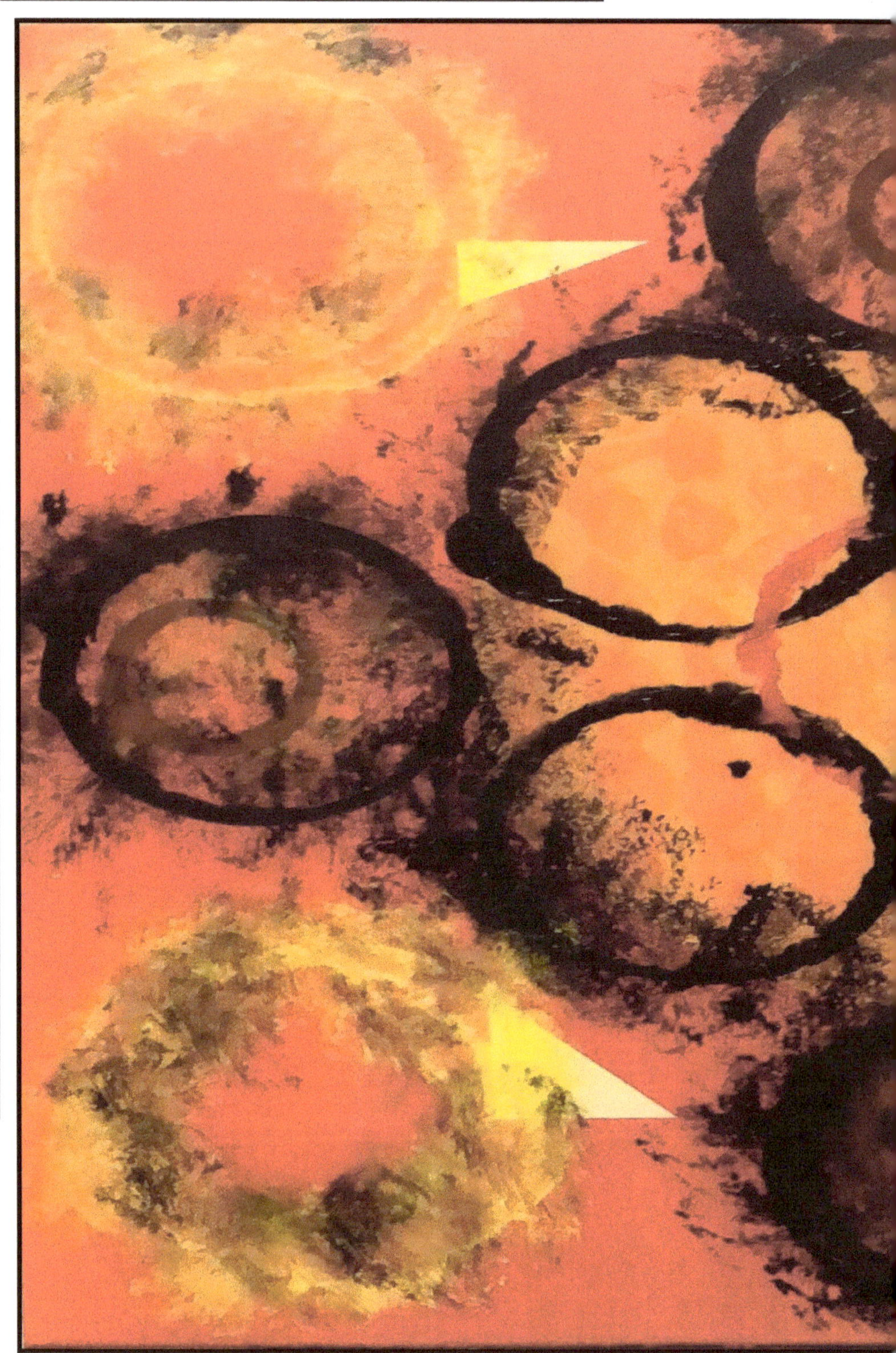

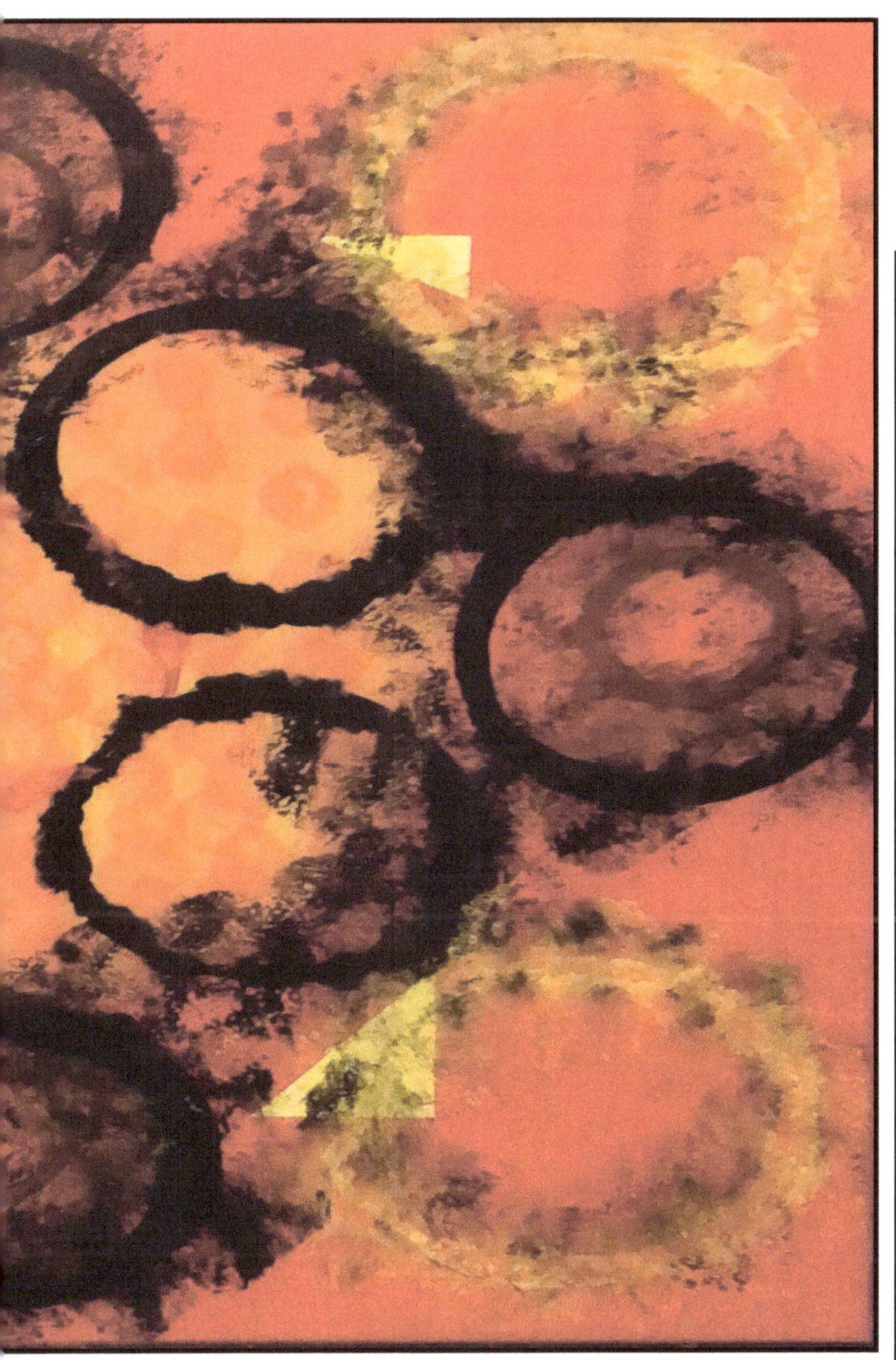

transformation of a door set ablaze

Bria Boecker

plucked from the ashes of a farmhouse
carved and intricate like cracks on her palm
white paint peeling
the color of innocence, weak adhesion.

Repurposed   Refinished   Redone

planted in the bedroom of a girl
twiggy, grimy fingers tearing away
strips of paint, letting them fall
to the speckled carpet.

charred wood beneath, unveiled
history of a door, surface gazing
towards new purpose.

Old becomes New becomes Old

thinks the girl who has now sprouted tall

tree turned to door then
reborn, shadow stretching over
her life, she wonders
had it noticed the transformation?

saw slicing through its trunk
morphing itself into a door
catching on fire and waiting

to be moved to the room
where it could watch the girl

Grow and Leave and Return

her green irises, hawk–like
in nature, opened from the sight
of foreign skies, distant lands
offering, abundant nutrients.

flesh no longer rooted
in a room, once containing

an entire world in the palm
of her hand.

Remember   Release   Revitalize

lengthy fingers tracing
splintered wood, leaning
tender lips against the damage.

surface-level kiss
on innocence now faded,
girl sealed to door, recognizing
her flourish.

Vines

Walter Kwong

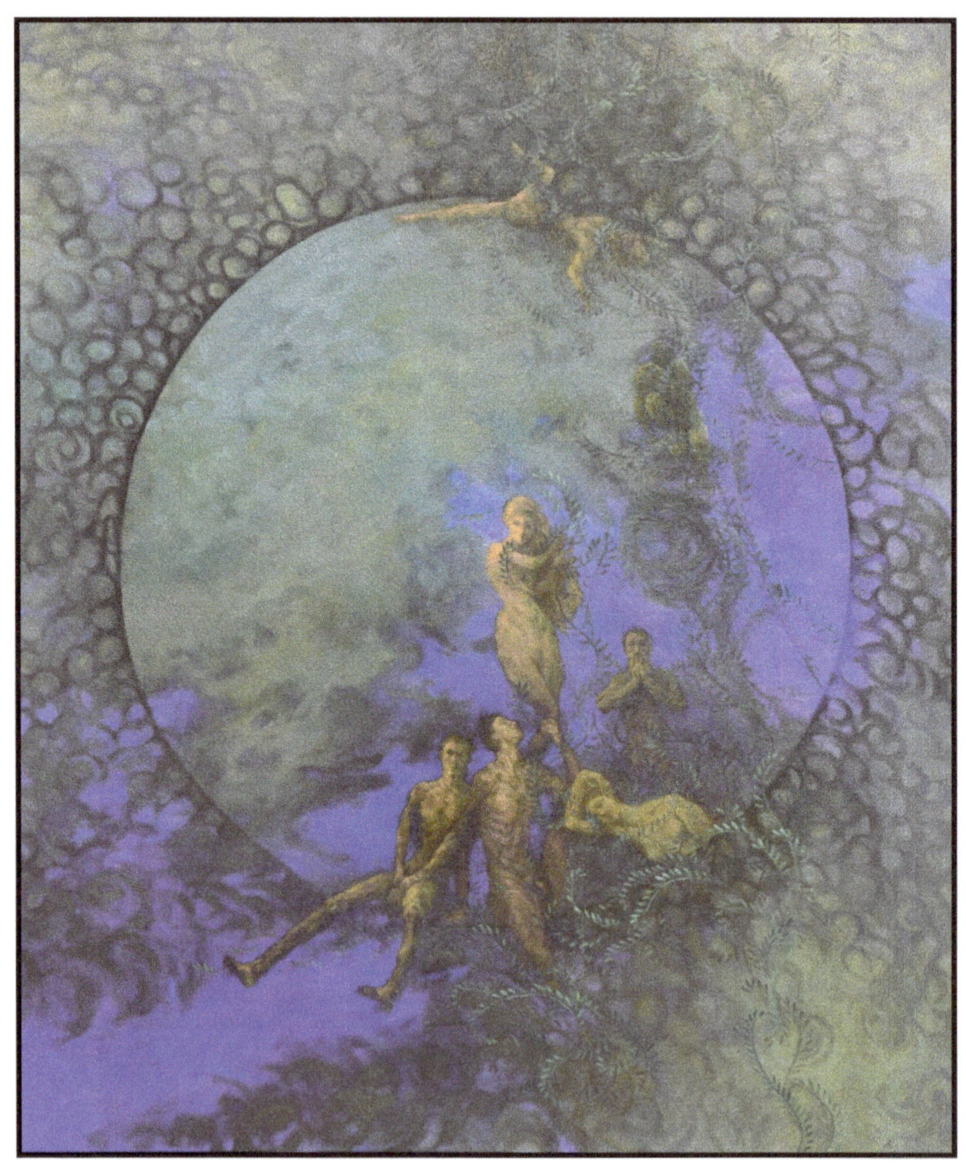

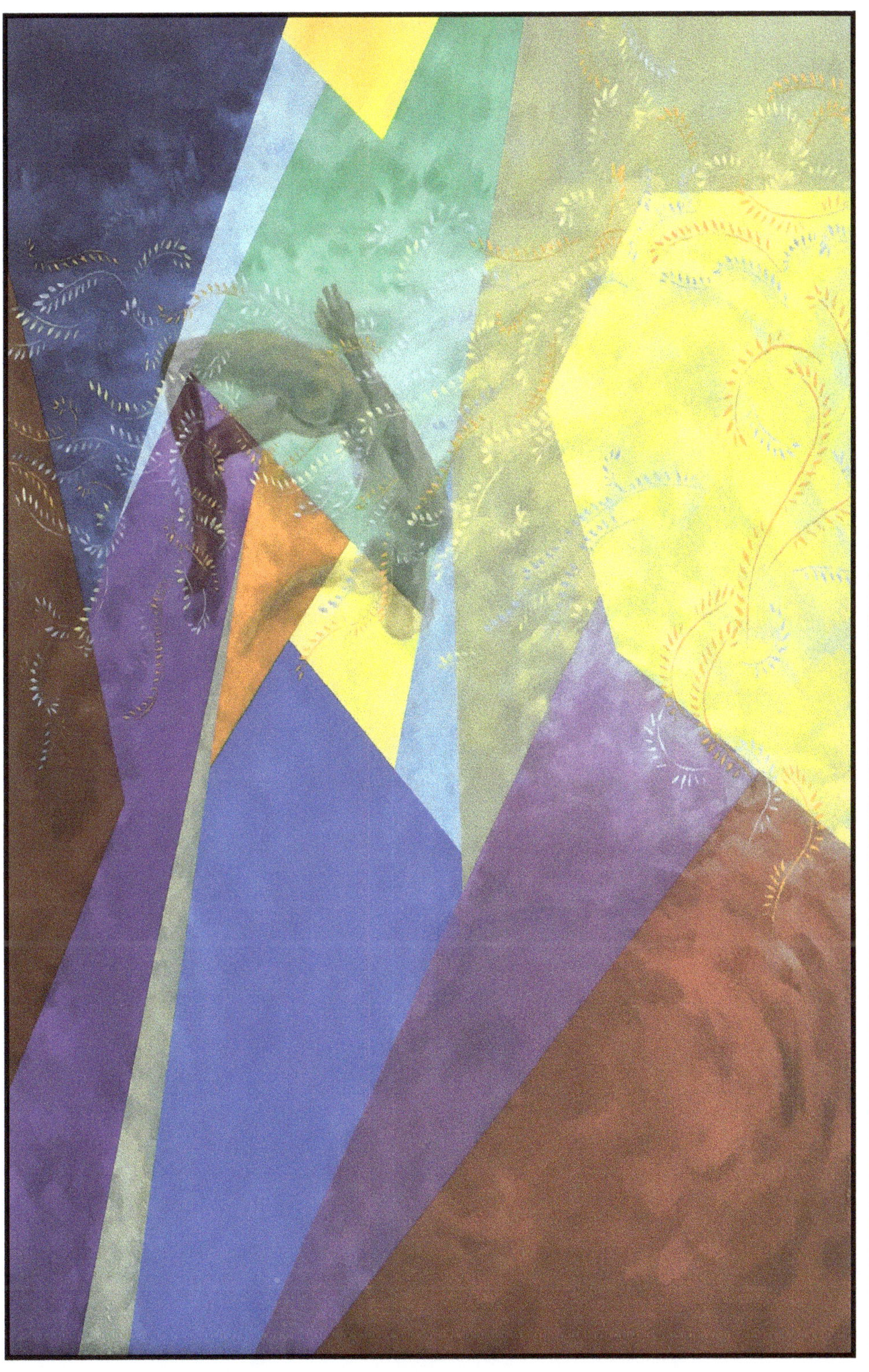

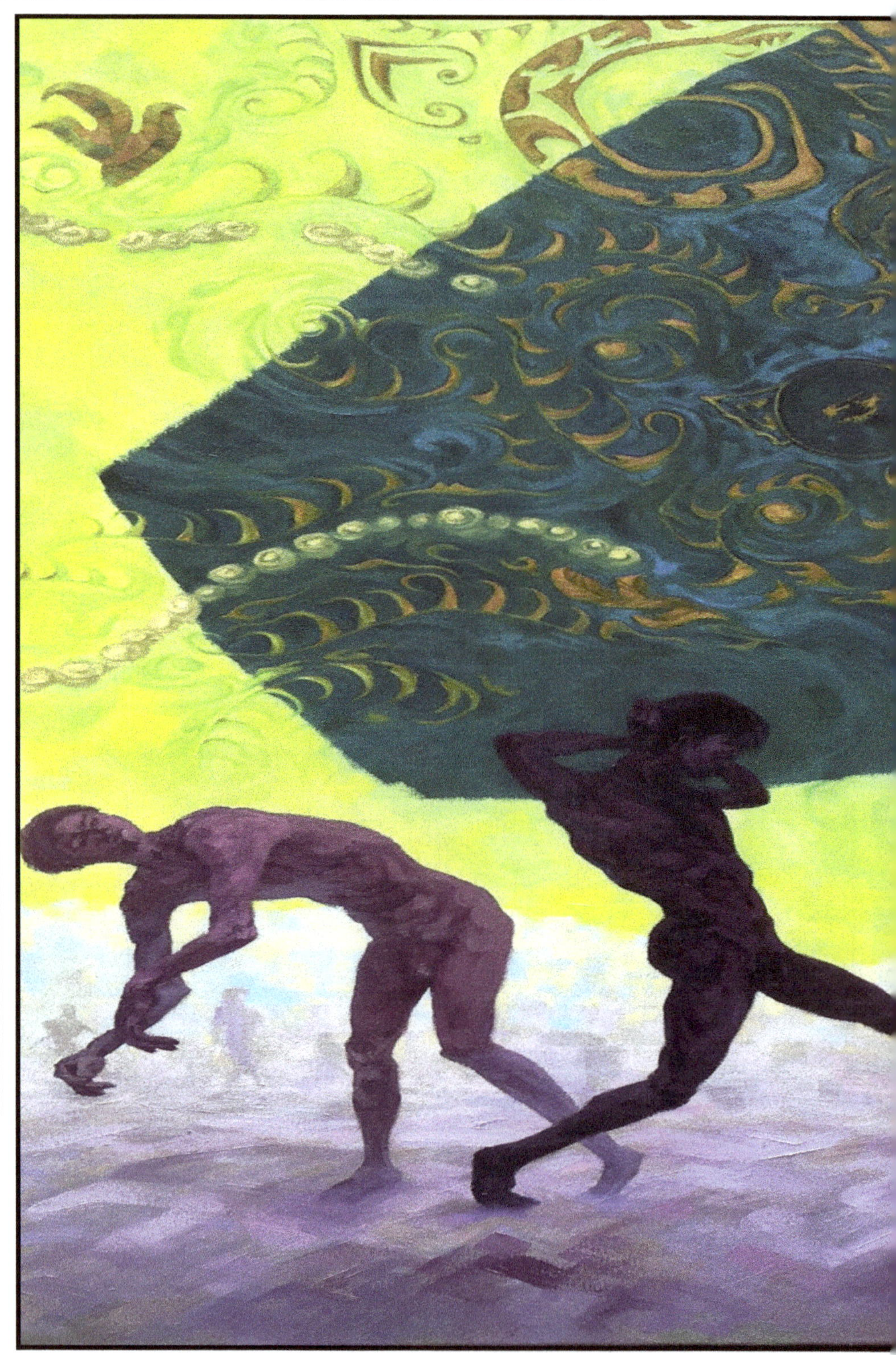

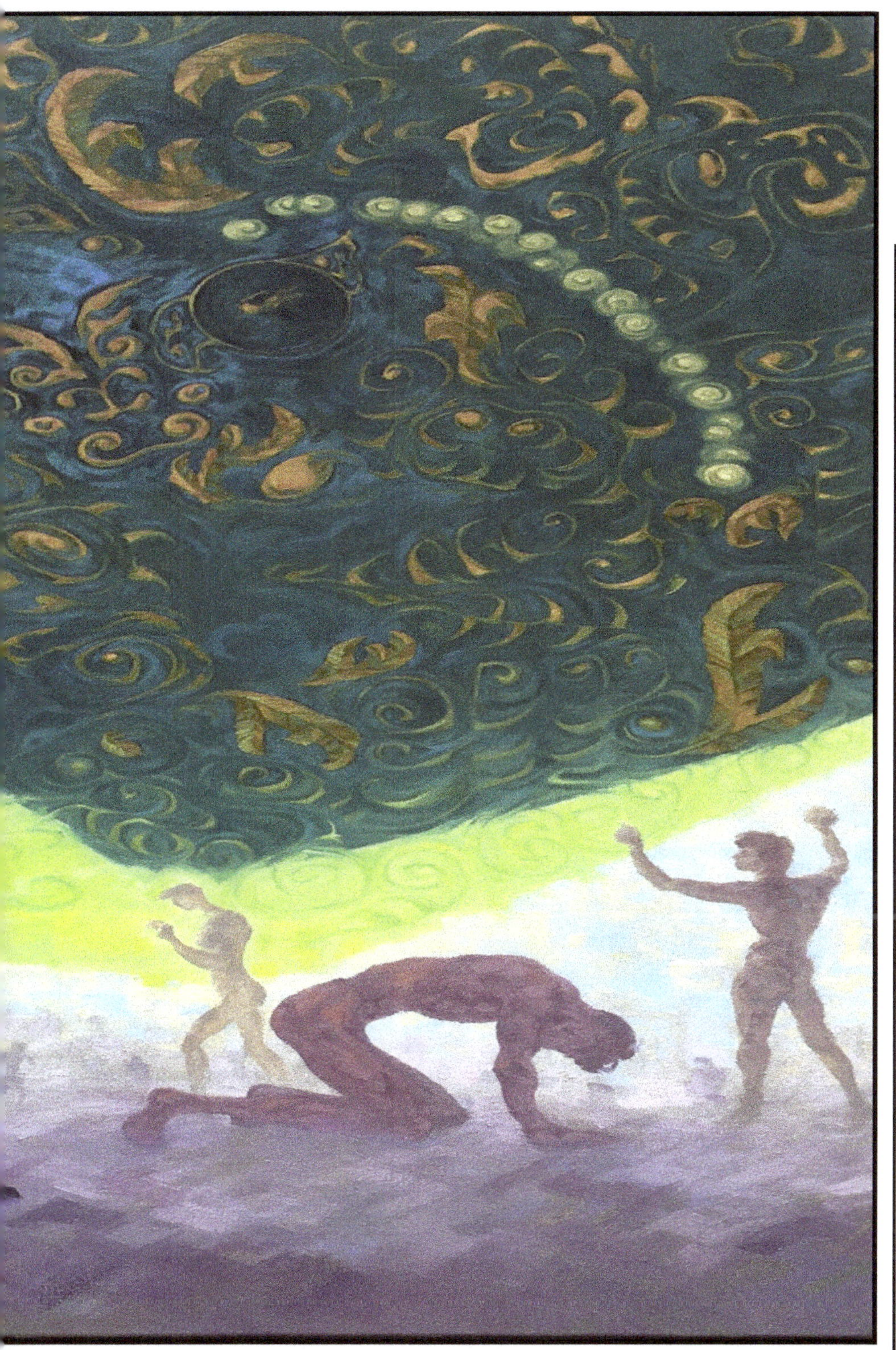

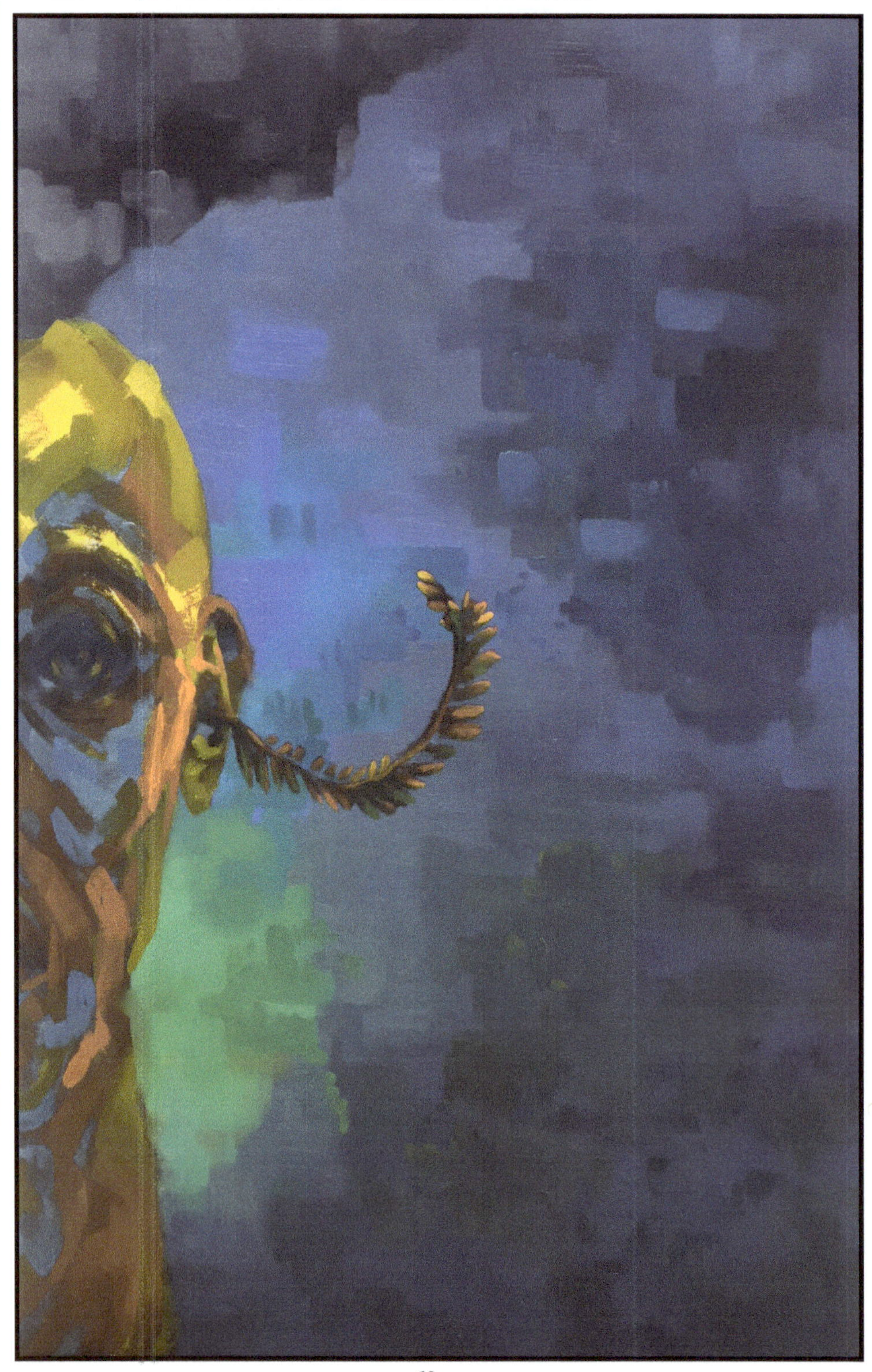

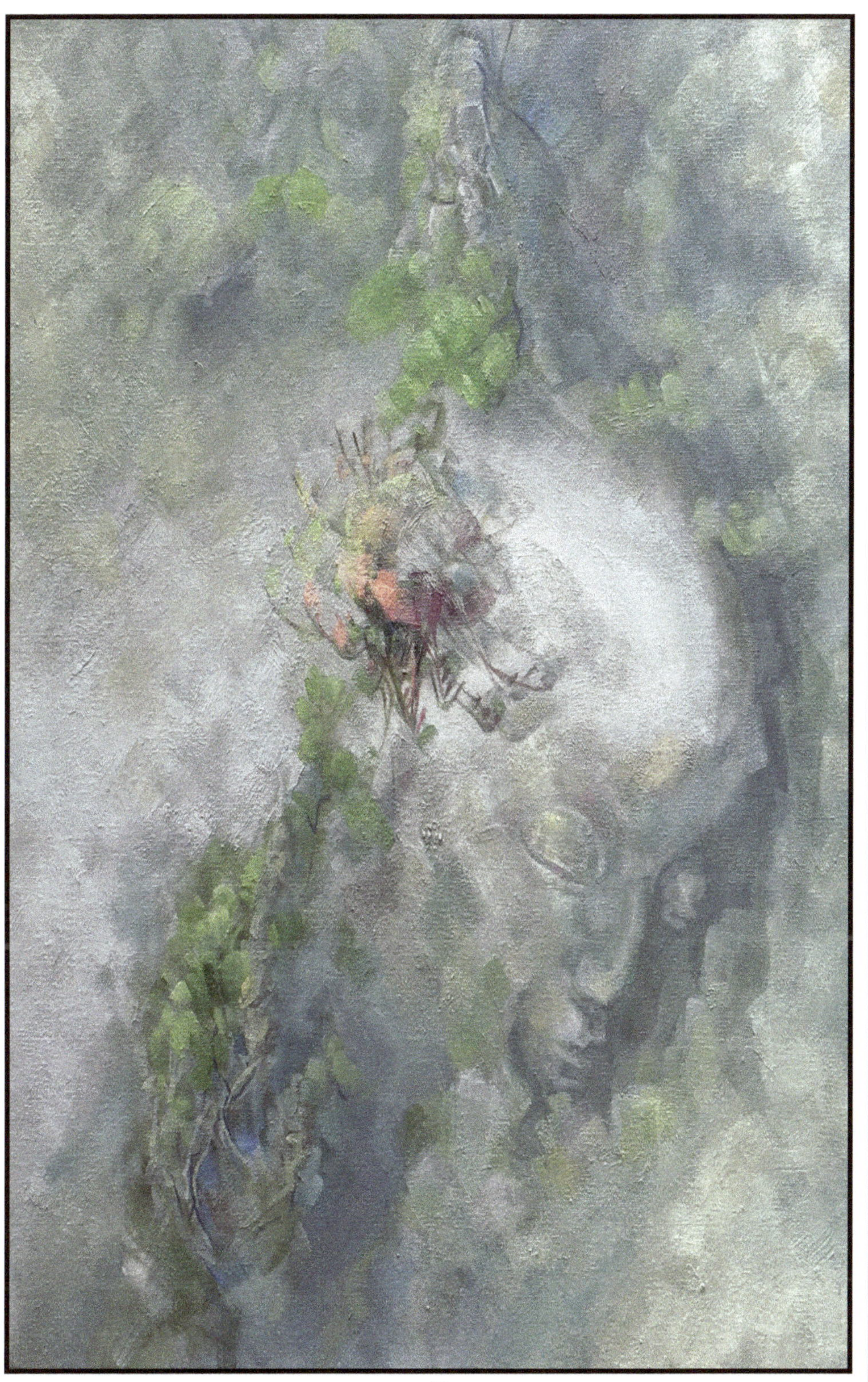

Midlight

Brian Udall

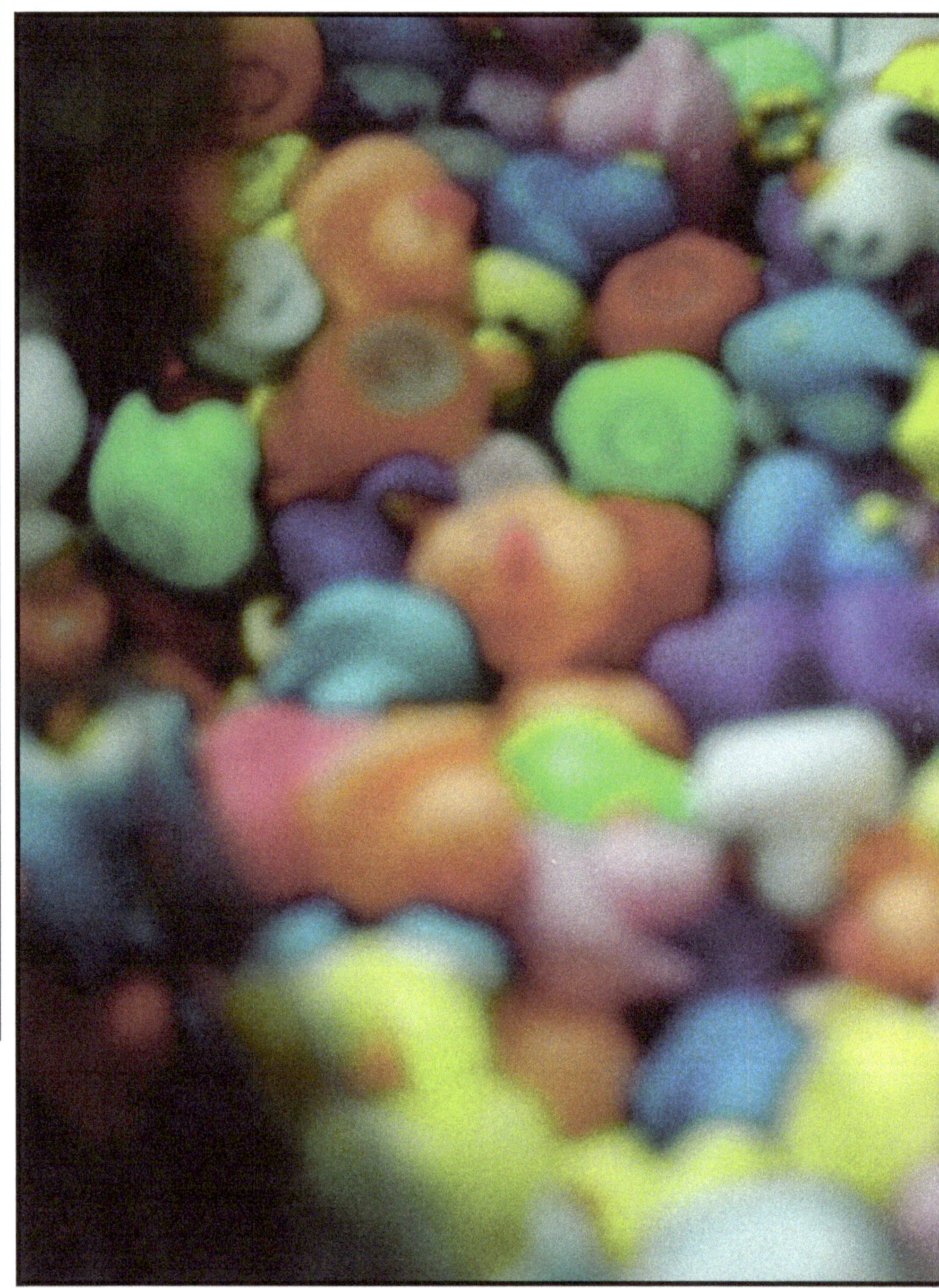

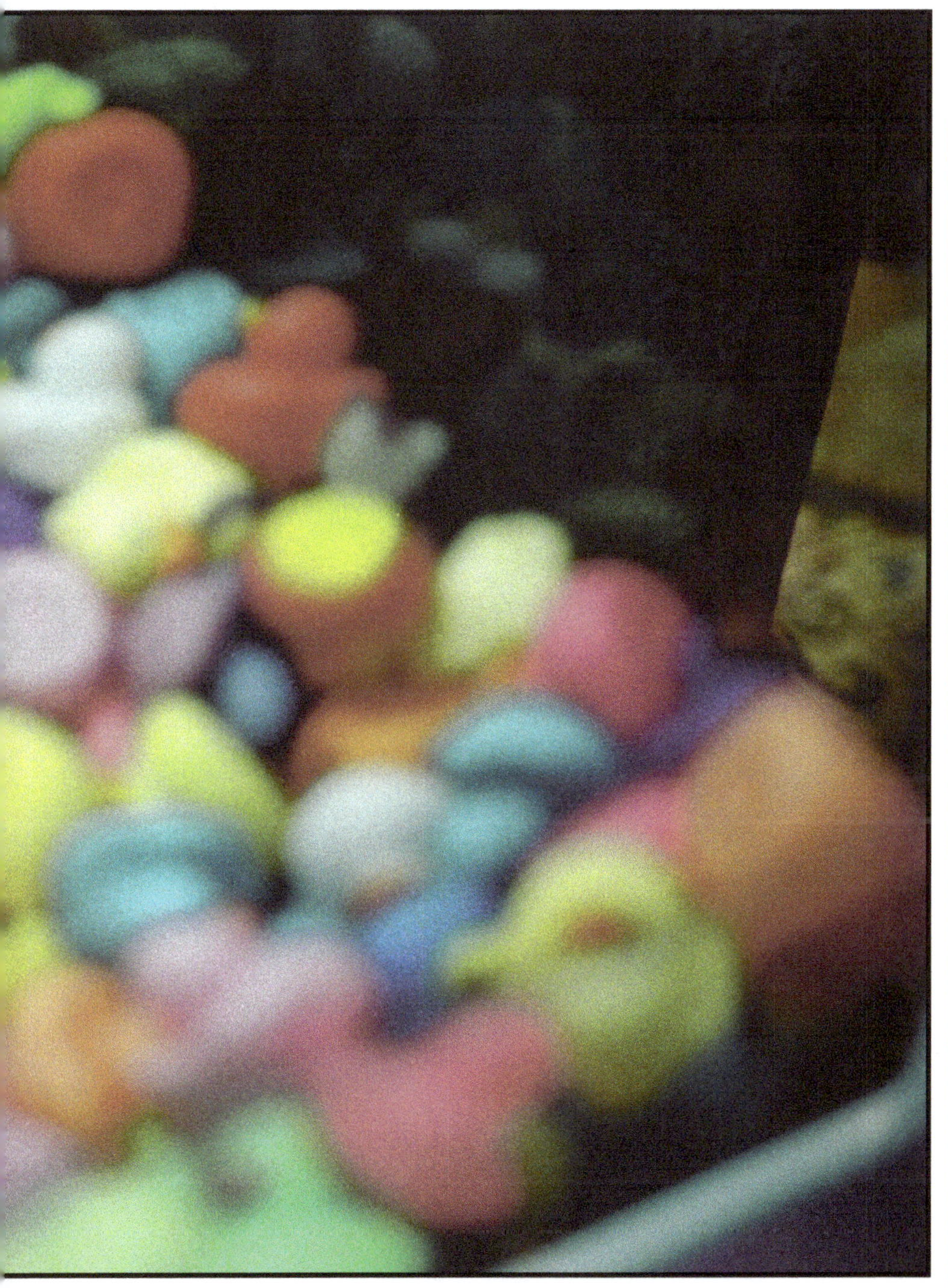

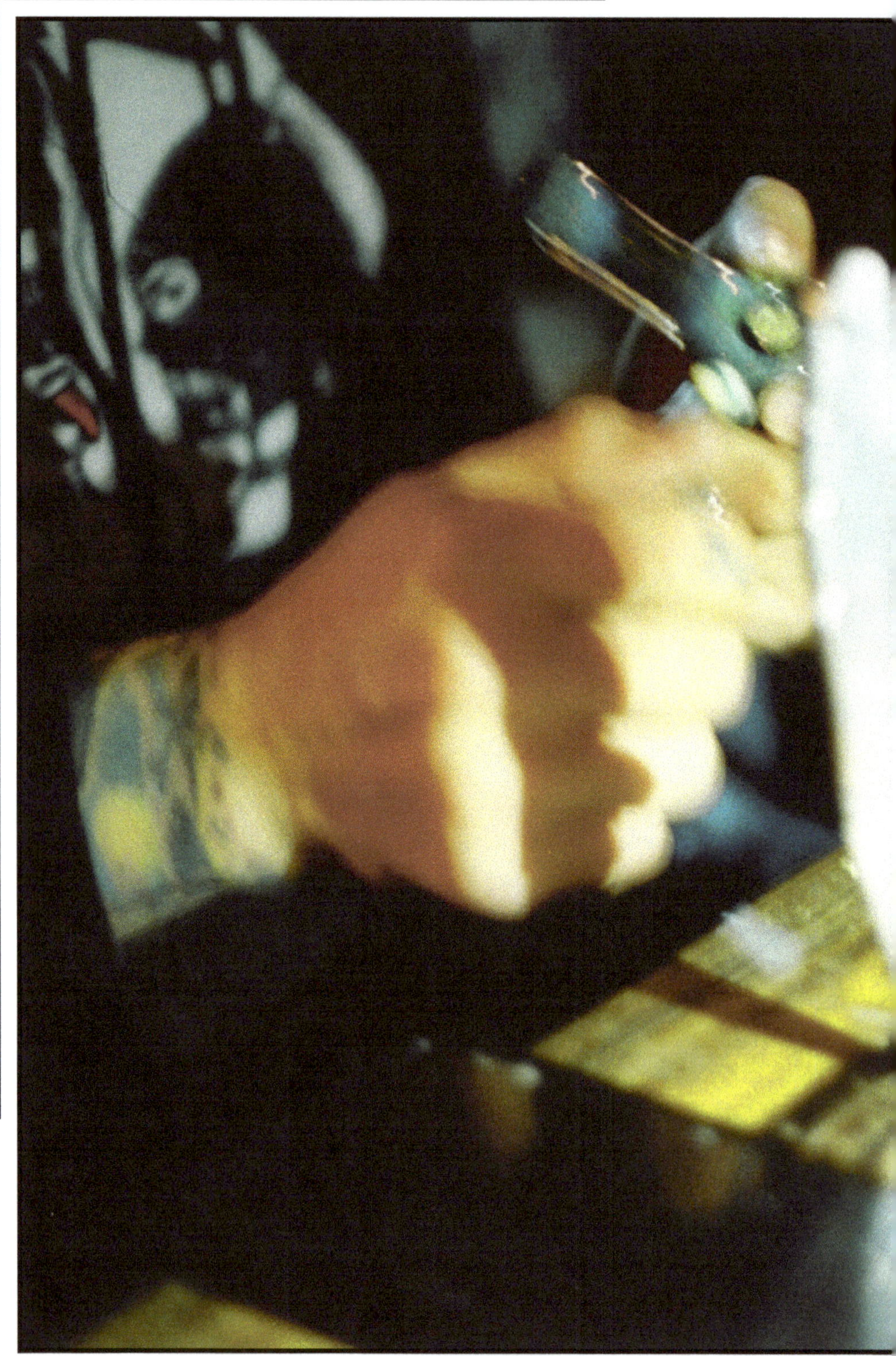

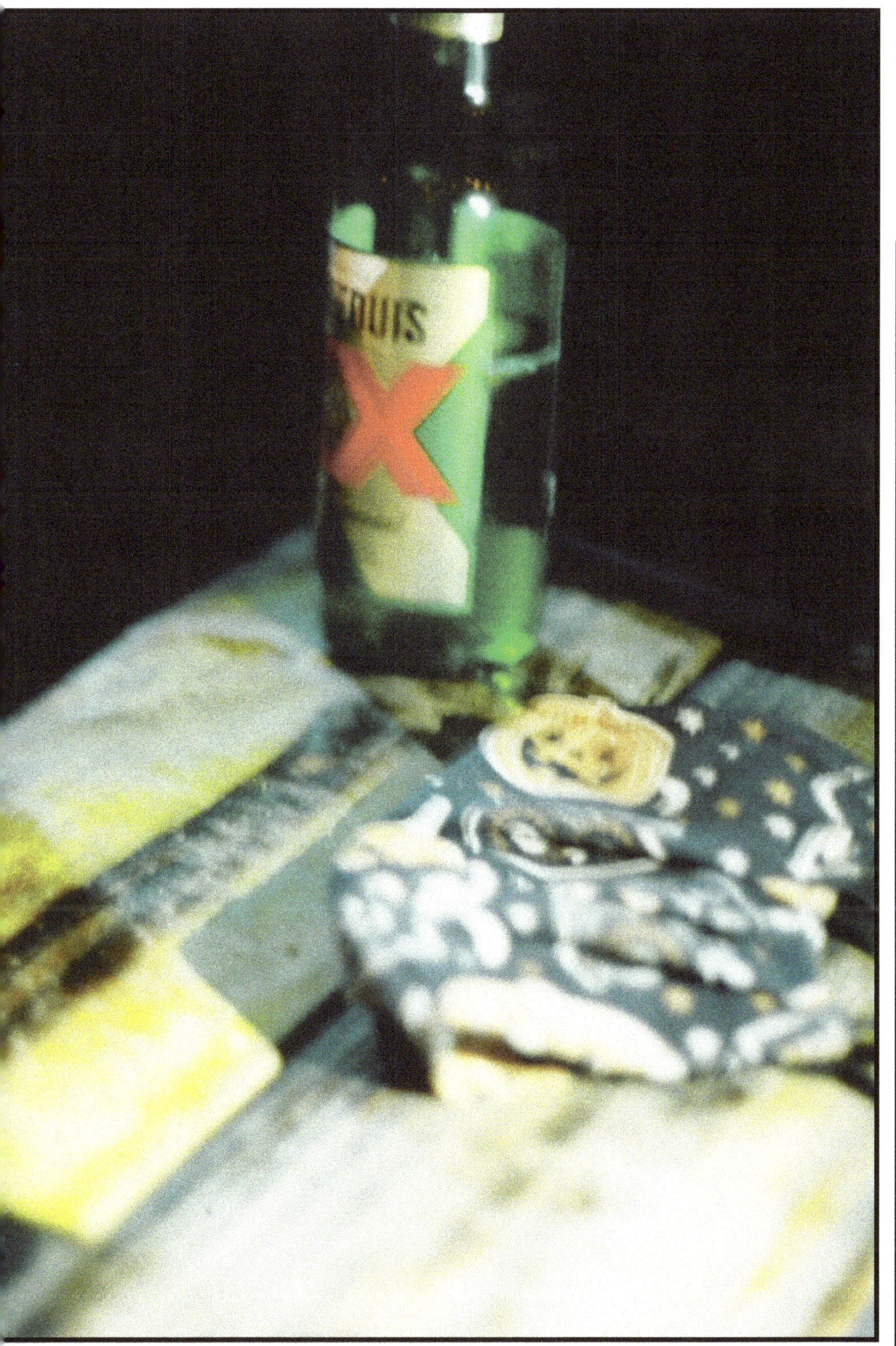

OUIS

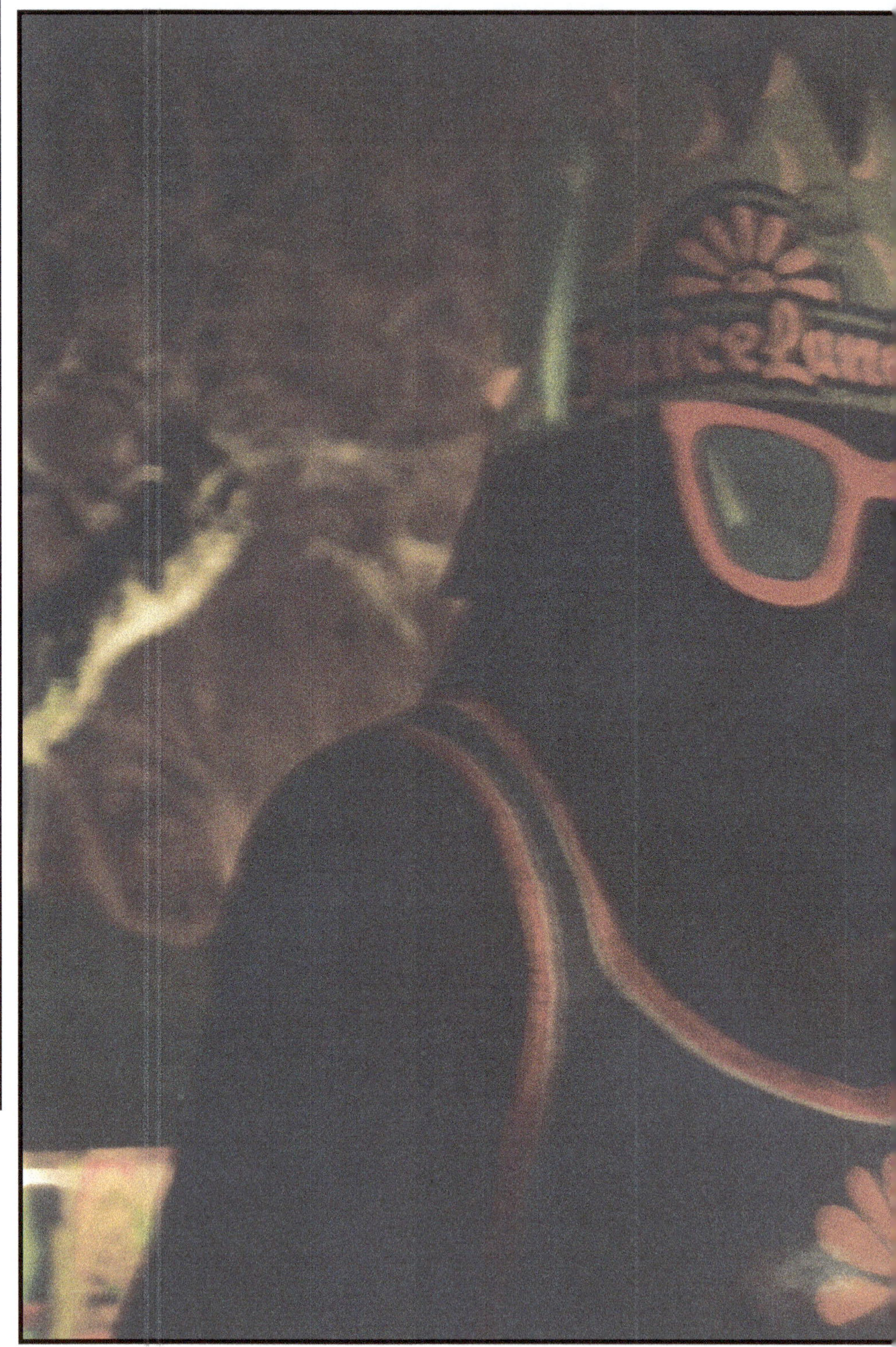

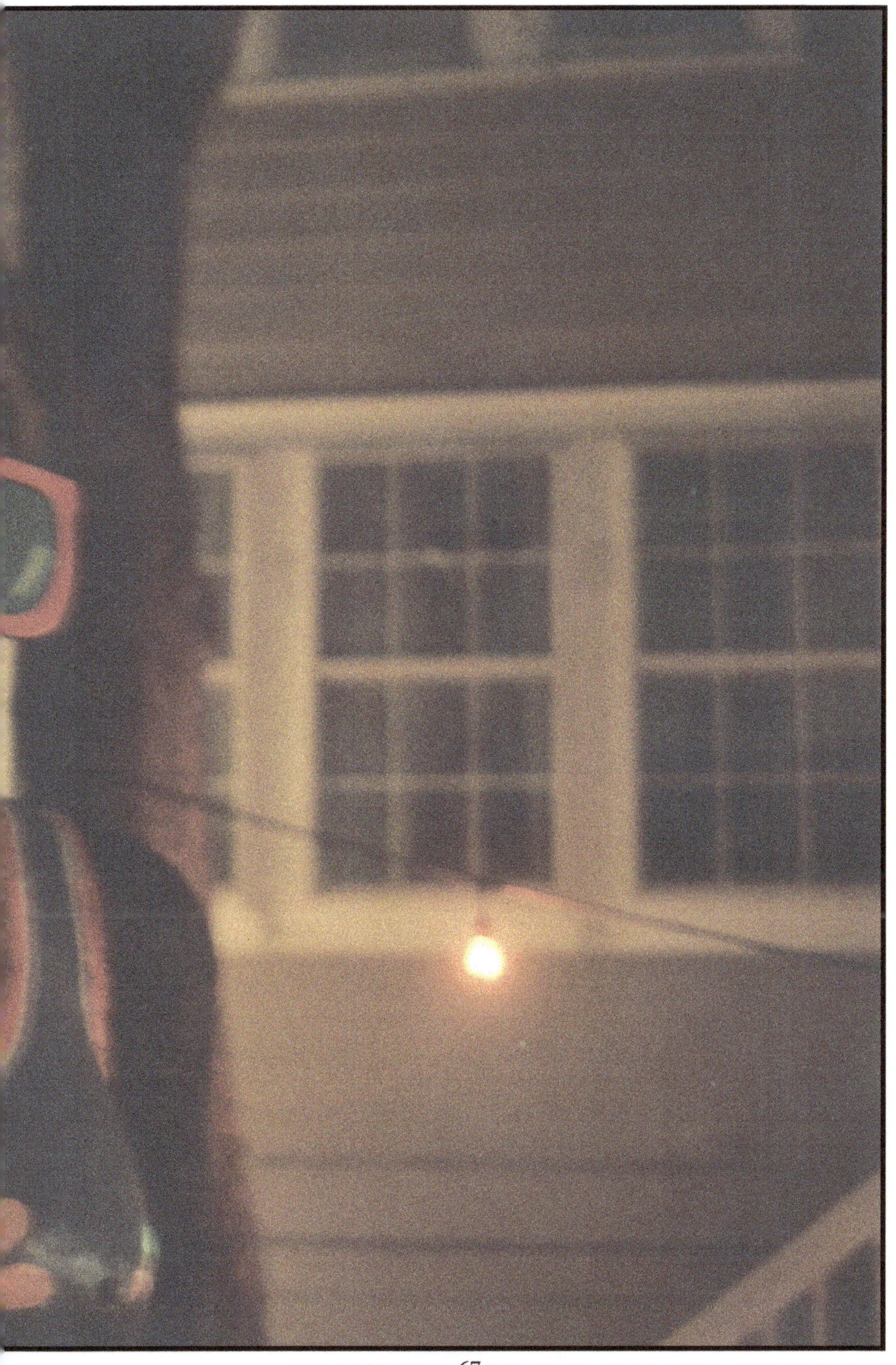

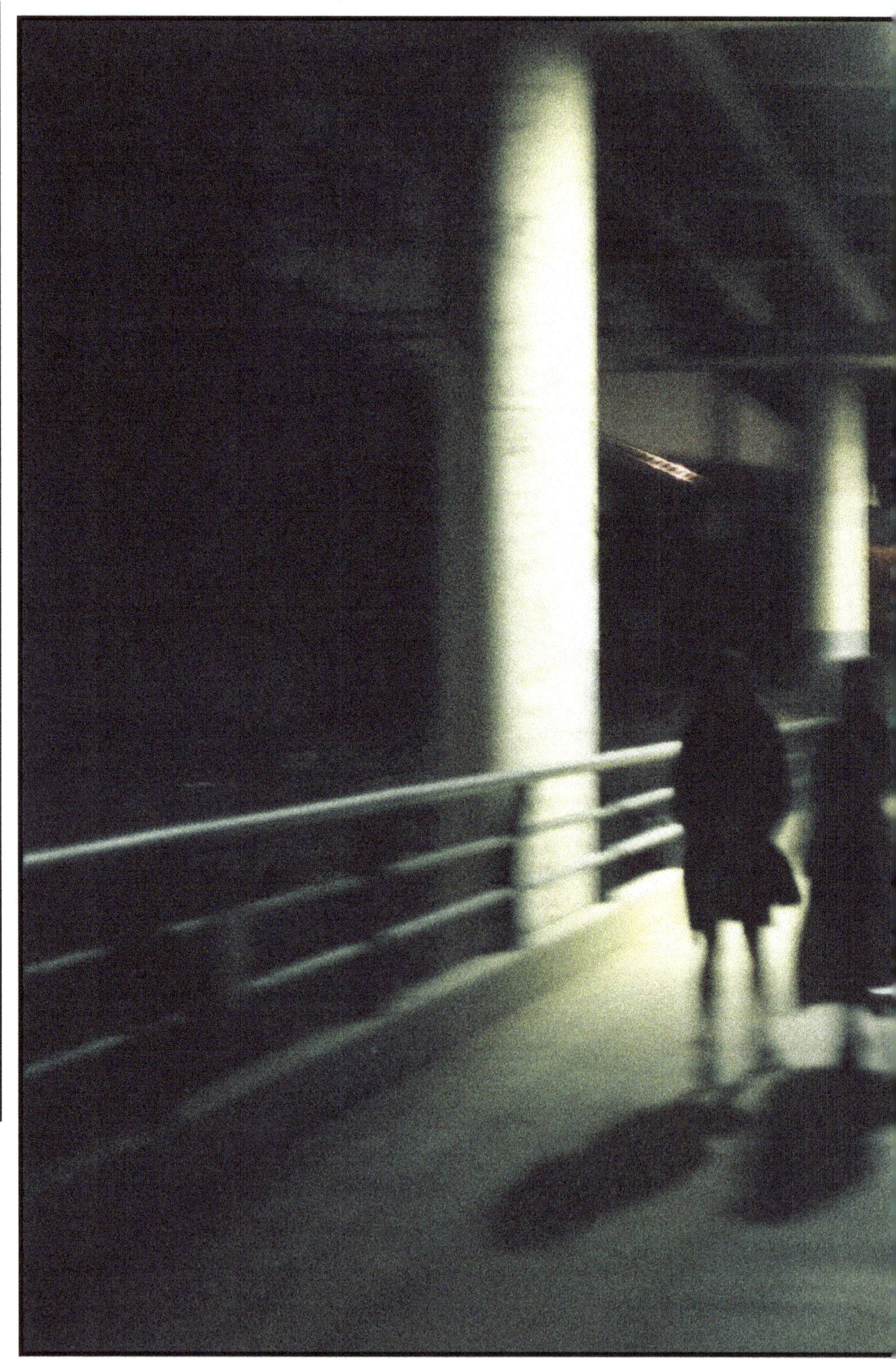

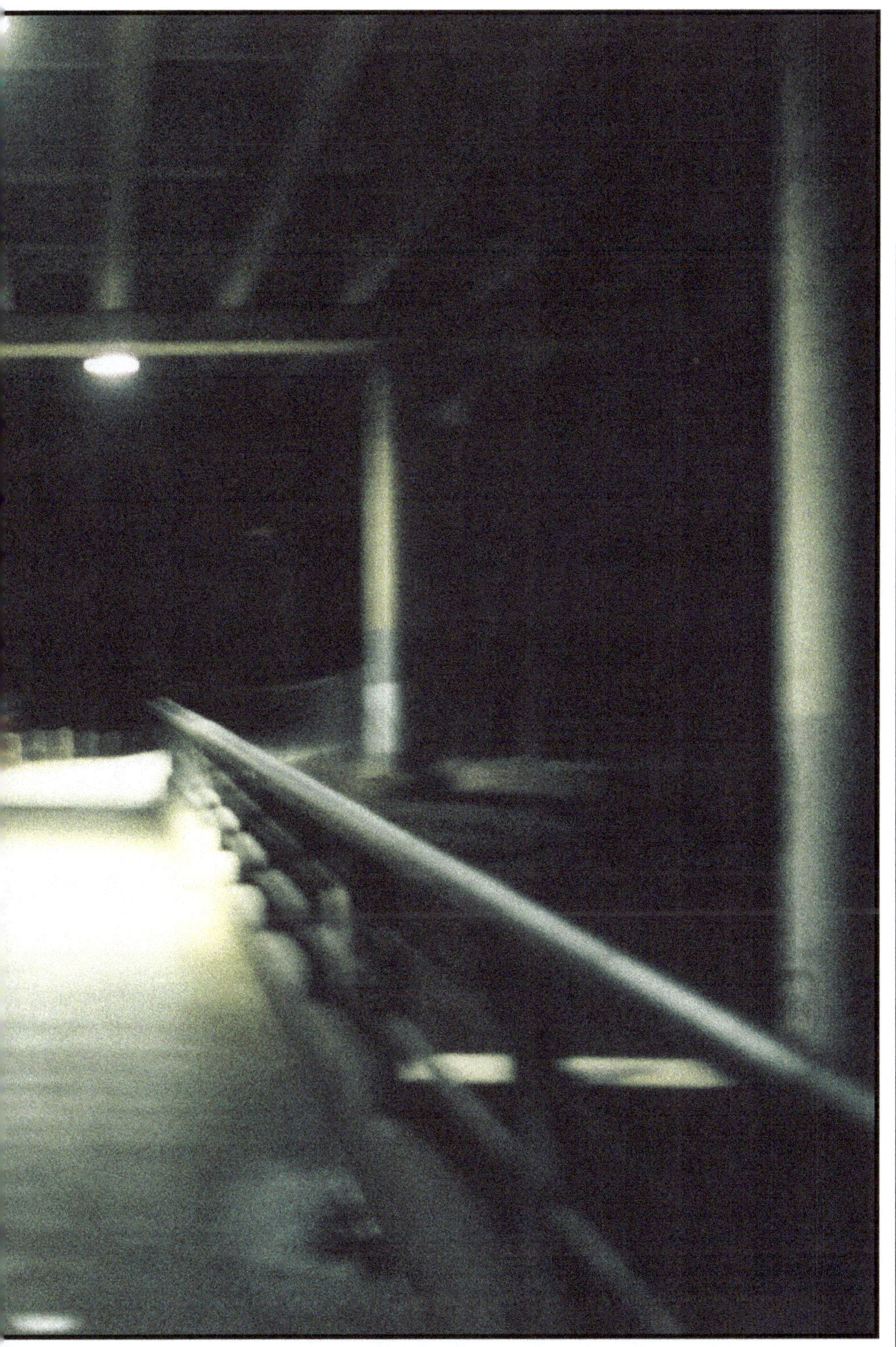

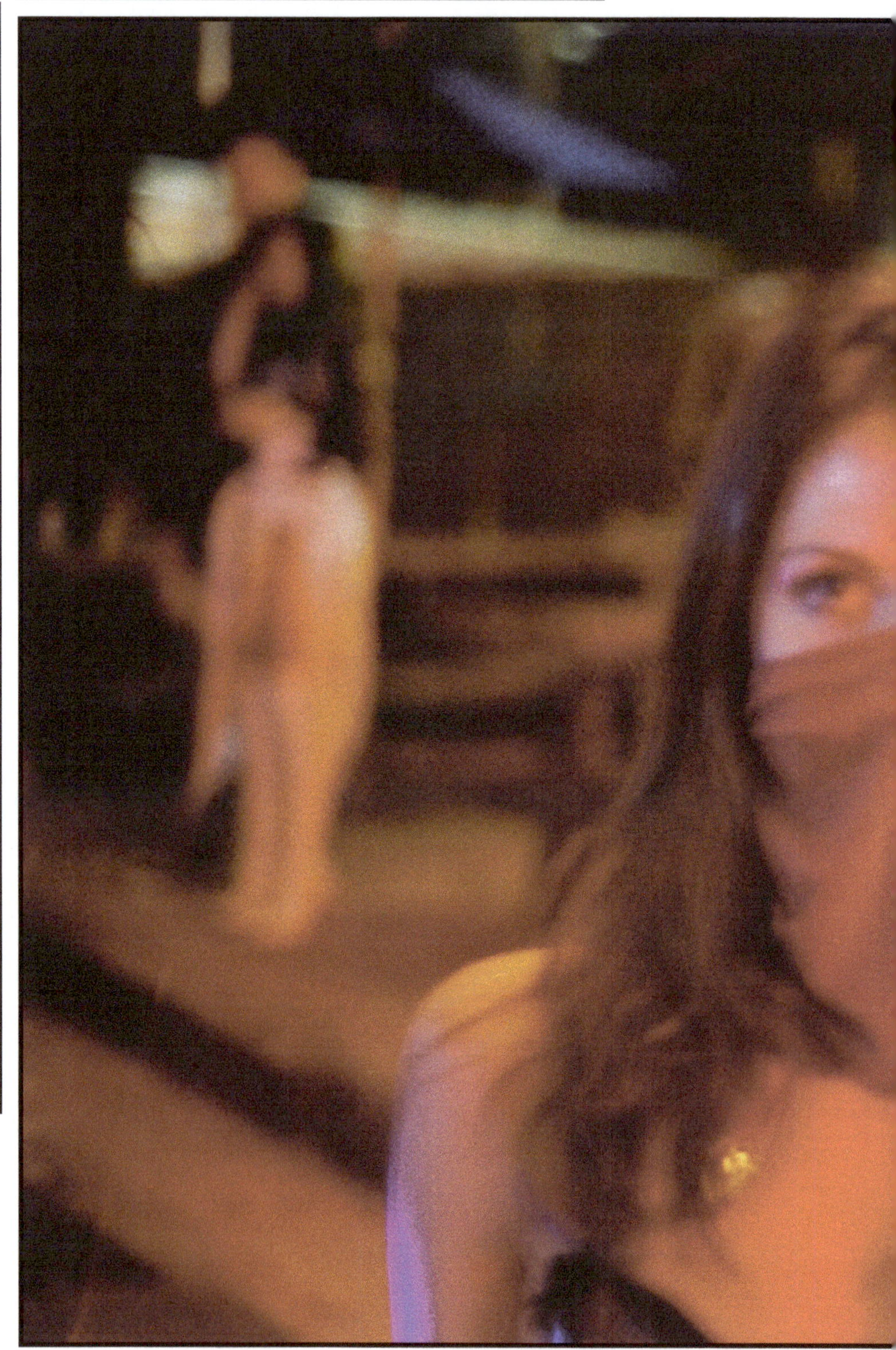

year of

Lisa Cantwell

impasse and circumstance in search of a blowhole
year of sonata in the key of goddamn
awful year of cosmic rebellion and karmic
reckoning of masked random anomie
of sexist abandon year of civil fatigue
at its peak and pine year of hindsight
of bombast and firestorm in burnt orange year
of ratatat infographic of unlucky numbers
crawling on all fours at sixes and sevens year
of surrender of howl and beg for table scraps
for mercy year of sick as a dog eat dog
whistle dog tired to the knick knack paddywhack
let's not put a label on this year yet but
can i be a feminist and still call you bitch

My Retirement Announcement

Michael Baker

It is with a heavy heart that I announce my retirement from the world of counterfeit prehistoric fossil smuggling. I understand this will come as a shock to my co-conspirators and law enforcement foils alike, and for that reason I feel an explanation is in order.

I trust you'll indulge me as I recount my humble beginnings as a grifter. Yes, it's true—I started out as a scammer, a chiseler, a real old fashioned confidence man. The Tallahassee Shuffle, the Two-Penny Turnover, the Hand It Over or I'll Cut You—sure, I ran all the classic cons. But my favorite swindle was convincing an unsuspecting mark to let me into his home by telling him my car broke down and I needed his phone to call a tow truck. Then, when the mark least suspected it, I'd steal his phone and run away to hide in the bushes near my broken-down car until the tow truck arrived. The ruse only worked because my marks were arrogant enough to try to help a person in need. So it's true what they say: you can't con an honest man.

Anyway, one day my Subaru blew a gasket in a nice neighborhood. Perfect, I thought, another opportunity to find a mark and get my hands on his phone. I knocked on a door, and some dopey mark answered and invited me in. Little did I know I would end up with more than just a near-obsolete piece of used consumer electronics. Quite a bit more, indeed. I know what you're thinking, but no—it wasn't that my mark ended up having one of those cool headset phones. Not even I'm that lucky. As I entered the foyer—like I said, this neighborhood was pretty swanky— a slab of gray stone caught my eye. It wasn't the stone itself (though I must admit it was nice, as far as stones go), it was the white etchings on the stone that intrigued me. I'm no paleontologist, but I could tell these were cave drawings—*prehistoric* cave drawings.

Imagine my surprise when the foolish mark told me this brilliant piece of prehistory was a fake. He then showed me others, a whole garage full of poorly-assembled imitation artifacts of times gone by. That's right—this dumb, unsuspecting mark was involved with the distribution of counterfeit prehistoric fossils! As you can probably guess, I didn't steal his phone. Instead, I used the phone to call a tow truck then paid the tow truck driver fifty bucks to distract the mark while I stole all of his counterfeit fossils. I may have been one stolen phone short of my quota, but I was officially in the counterfeit prehistoric fossil smuggling game.

I soon made connections in the shadowy world of counterfeit fossil smuggling. When you've got a product that hot the major players have a way of finding you. I won't bore you with the details of my meteoric rise to prominence, I trust you've heard them many times before. As my renown grew, so did the risks I became willing to take. I was soon flying to Cleveland three or four times a month. (Few people realize Cleveland is the hub of the international counterfeit fossil smuggling community. Makes perfect sense once you know, doesn't it?) Eventually I met Tom—better known in the smuggling game as Tommy Pastrami, Ol' Tom Hustle, or, for the most part, Thomas Williamson. Tom became my most trusted accomplice—my stickman, a real shill's shill, the genuine article (a rare thing in the world of counterfeit fossils).

Recently Tom and I had a big score lined up—a shipment of manufactured Dilophosaurus eggs from Northern India. As any counterfeit fossil man worth his salt can tell you, Northern India is the Cleveland of the Far East. You may recall the Dilophosaurus from *Jurassic Park*, he's the weird dinosaur that spits goo all over the guy who played Newman on *Seinfeld*. I always loved *Seinfeld*, and I was not above capitalizing off the popularity of the dinosaur that spit on and ate Newman. Suffice it to say, when I heard about the shipment of fake eggs I really wanted to smuggle them. *Illegally* smuggle them, mind you.

So we're at the Cleveland airport unloading our shipment, hoisting big boxes of fake dinosaur eggs into my Subaru. I couldn't help but notice Tom was sort of slacking. I was about to ask, "Hey Tom, what gives? Why don't you help me load these counterfeit prehistoric fossils into my Subaru so we can get a move on? What we're doing is, after all, illegal." But I never got the chance. What happened next has altered the course of my life for the past nine hours.

"Freeze dirtbag!" Tom shouted.

Now, Tom had called me a dirtbag many times, but somehow I knew this time was different. Maybe it was the way he pointed a cocked revolver at me as he spoke – I may be just a simple internationally-renowned smuggler, but I'm savvy enough to know that's not the sort of thing a fella does just fooling around. I thought of all the times I'd seen Tom wearing his *FBI: Female Body Inspector* t-shirt, we always had a good laugh. Who could've guessed he'd turn out to be an actual FBI agent? In hindsight I realize there was nothing ironic about the shirt—indeed, I'd caught Tom examining the female form on more than one occasion. How could I have been so blind? Take it from me: never trust an accomplice with a .gov email address.

So that's it. Busted. Somehow I always knew it would end this way (either this way, or with not getting caught—I always considered that a possibility, too). I've always been a big fan of *The Shawshank Redemption*, so you might think I'm pretty jazzed about the idea of spending time in a real-life prison. Well, you'd be mistaken. I guess it's true that crime doesn't pay (if you get caught, I mean; if you don't get caught it pays quite handsomely). So I've decided to hang it all up. Sure, I'll miss the lifestyle—the opulence, the glamour, the intrigue. But most of all, I'll miss the discounts on counterfeit prehistoric fossils.

To my esteemed co-conspirators around the globe: know that even now, as I sit at the Office of the U.S. Attorney prepared to accept a plea agreement to avoid prison by testifying against all of you, I think only of the good times. Maybe we'll meet again, and if we do I hope my assumed identity and extensive plastic surgery will allow me to avoid identification until I'm out of reach of your ever-expanding criminal empire.

I remain, as always, your humble servant in counterfeit prehistoric fossil smuggling,

J. Montgomery Malloy, III

P.S. If the Feds are reading this, please don't seize the ornamental sand dollars in the guest bathroom of my condo. I'm pretty sure they're real.

I'M THE MINUTES TO MIDNIGHT DOOMSDAY CLOCK

AND I NEED TO RETHINK MY SOCIAL MEDIA STRATEGY

Linda Schlossberg

Doomsday Clock Says World Remains '100 Seconds' From Disaster

The Bulletin of the Atomic Scientists said the clock's position would remain unchanged from 2020, when its hands were set as close as they had ever been to a catastrophic "midnight"...The bulletin's Science and Security Board, which is composed of nuclear and climate experts and other scientists, meets twice a year to discuss how world events should dictate where the clock's hands will fall. –The New York Times, January 27, 2021

Hey. DC here. So this is awkward and I know you'd rather not think about it, but the thing is, we're still 100 seconds from The End.

I didn't want it to be 100 seconds. I told the Board, that just SOUNDS weird— no one says "100 seconds from"—they say 90 seconds or 60 seconds. They're all, oh, 100 seconds has a nice ring to it. Apocalyptic stuff is very on trend and you're going to blow up like crazy. Blow, up, get it?

But no, all anyone cares about is Bernie's mittens and Champ and Major... Have you seen how much traction those guys get? It's like they take a piss in the Rose Garden and everyone loses their shit and I'm all, HELLO THE WORLD IS DYING and no one cares.

I told them, we gotta up my socials. No one ever says, look at this cute meme of the Doomsday Clock on the moon... or, here he is with a baby panda...

Get me on twitter, instagram. I'm a freakin clock, put me on tik-tok!

We need clickbait. Get some eyeballs on me! World's hottest timepieces, or... I dunno. I'm working on it, ok? Put some Bernie mittens on my hands.

What about a GIF of me with Big Ben? A Doomsday emoji? An app where you can put your face on my face?

The problem is these days it's all about likes and nobody likes me. That fucker the Pantone Color of the Year is all, oh, I'm going to the Vanity Fair Party at Fashion Week and I have no idea what to wear—Will I see you there? Even though he knows I never get invited anywhere.

Whatever. I don't need to be popular. I think I'm just exhausted, honestly.

People tell me I'm wound too tight, that I should chill, take some Xanax. Watch some Netflix. The world's already depressing enough, and it's not like I have anything new to say. I'm an Old. My image and messaging have stayed pretty much the same since... Let's see.... When did I start this gig?

1947.

When I started, Alfred Einstein was on the Board. Yes, that Alfred Einstein. And all this time, I've only wanted one thing—

Your attention.

They say time marches on, but I can't march—I'm kind of stuck here. So I need the rest of you to go out and march and protest and write to your representatives and tweet and post and spread the word, ok? Make some noise—because as far as I can tell, we're running out of time.

And a cute picture of a kitten in a bell tower never hurts. Just saying.

Privatization

Photography by Sofie Rosalien Deen

Poem by Katie Kurtz

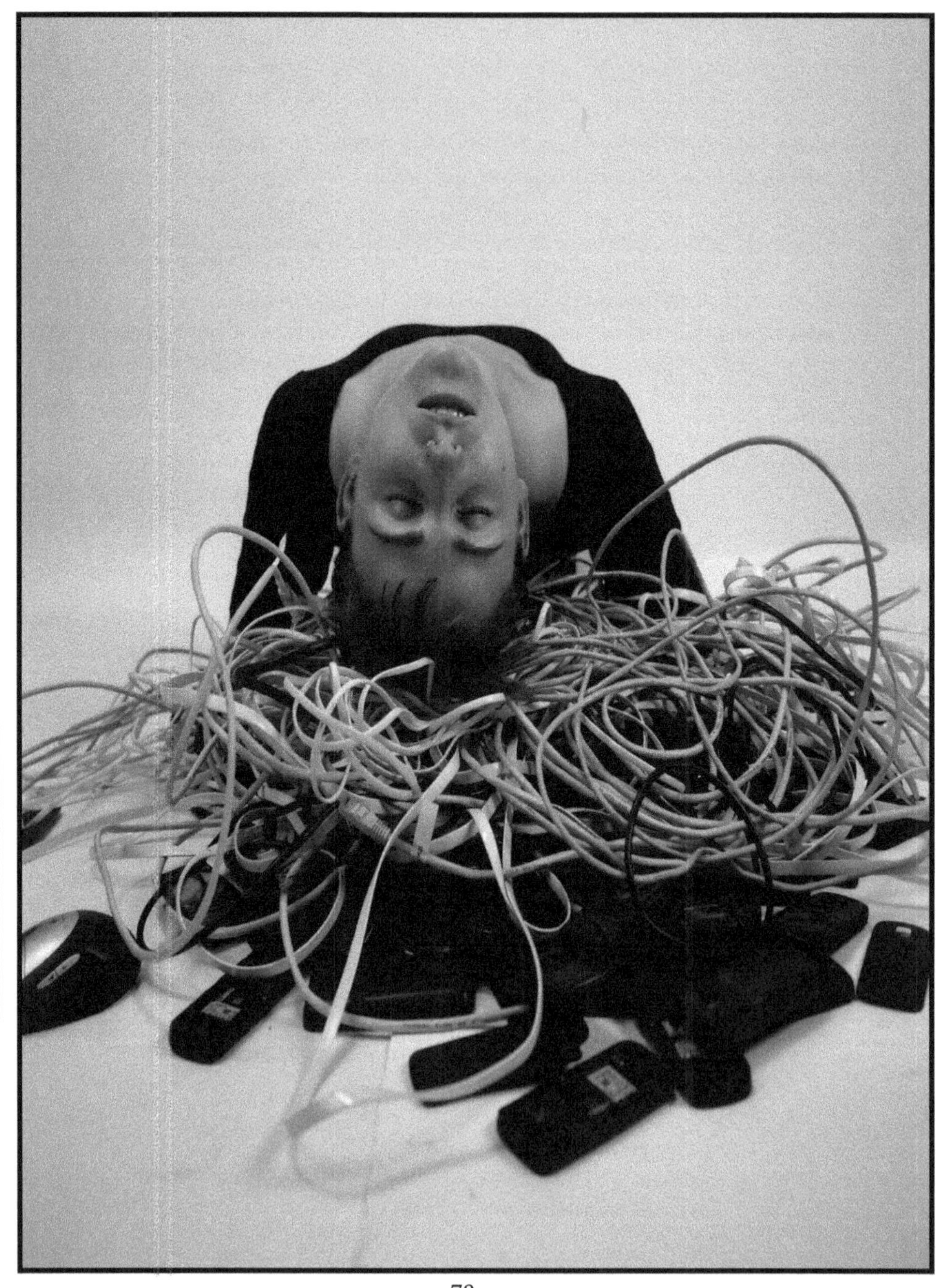

Polyvalence gets the best of me –
such lame attempts at meaning more. Clearly.

I'm special, though, as special as the four
billion, ninety seven million, fifty

eight thousand, three hundred forty
three others born the same year as me.

Fight apathy. Or don't. Tear the roof off
the sucker. Or not. Diamond in the rough

or my heart, like yours, is solid black –
my innards coiled for miles and miles.

Online, our funny little homunculi
burn brilliant, as if lit by kliegs.

Turned on in networks, awash
in a sea of gigs and RAMs –

we're not the Alpha and the Omega but
byte-sized nanos with no room to swing a dead cat.

(God LOLs, God says whatevs,
God, of course, is totes dead.)

Who wants to be known by what they own?
At least millions, ticking toward eighty billion.

Possessed by possessions, my list is short:
laptop, iPod, cell phone, PIN, login, password, paper, pen...

In Order Of Appearance:

Gina Williams is a Portland, Oregon-based writer, visual artist, and gardener. Her writing and visual art have been featured most recently by The Inflectionist Review, River Teeth, The Esthetic Apostle, High Shelf Press, Okey-Panky, Carve, The Sun, Fugue, La Piccioletta Barca, and Great Weather for Media, among others. My full-length poetry collection, "An Unwavering Horizon" was published in May 2020. Learn more about her and my work at GinaMarieWilliams.com

K.G. Ricci has spent most of his seventy years in New York City where he currently lives and works. It has only been the last five years that he has devoted himself to the creation of his collage panels. Though not formally trained, Ken worked in the art department at the Strand Bookstore during his student years and it was there that he familiarized himself with the works of his favorite artists, including Bearden, di Chirico and Tooker. After a career in the music business and a decade of teaching in NYC schools, Ken began creating his own original artwork in earnest.
Ken's collage panels are strictly cut/paste paper on a hardboard base. As his work has evolved, he has added a hinged caption or title as an essential component of each panel. In a relatively short period of time, Ken's approach became more focused on the latent narrative possibilities of the medium and with that potential connection in mind, the size of the panels changed from the early 24" x 48" to the current 8"x 24". The smaller panels seem to perfectly suit the artist's degree of narration and it is only recently that Ken has brought the lessons learned on the small panels back to the larger surface with somewhat surprising results. Most recently, Ken has focused on creating collages on 6x9 black paper using a minimum of images to evoke or suggest a deeper narrative without title or caption. Ken has been fortunate to have a number of his panels from the series Hotel Kafka and Femma Dilemma appear at a number of themed exhibitions in both New York and California galleries.

Leanne Hoppe holds an MFA in poetry from Boston University. She works as a teacher, editor, and translator in Cleveland.

Shana Blatt is an emerging poet who holds a BA from Purchase College, where she studied Literature and Creative Writing. She is a collector of keychains and coping mechanisms.

Since 2014, Jamie Johnson (Birdee) has been capturing the female form through her photography. In her work she examines themes of femininity, strength, and grace, as well as exploring the healing element of water. Her journey began with self portraiture as a means of embodiment and empowerment, and has since shared that same experience with others through immersive portrait sessions and fine art imagery.

Amanda Shaw is a journalist in Greenville, SC. She found her love of storytelling while pursuing an English degree at Furman University. When she's not writing, she's volunteering with a local wildlife rescue or binge-watching documentaries with her husband and cat-child.

My name is Dave J.

Lauren Belmore is a person returning to writing after a depression induced hiatus. They hold a B.A. in Playwriting from the University of North Texas, where they have been involved in various poetry collectives in the DFW area. They currently work as a sous-chef during a global pandemic. They had hoped 2020 would be "their year", but quickly decided that they would just try again in 2021.

Jacqueline Rosenbaum is originally from "all over" New York, but moved to Boston in 2017 to pursue her MFA in Fiction from UMass Boston. Upon receiving her Master's in 2020, she began working as a marketing assistant at Macmillan Learning. Jacqueline Rosenbaum has had prose published in Haunted Waters Press (Fall 2018; granted Runner Up in Fiction contest), Adelaide Literary Magazine (April 2019), and the Merrimack Review (Spring 2020).

Doug Dabbs is an illustrator, comic book artist, and university professor who has taught visual storytelling in higher education for over a decade. His comic books and graphic novels have been published by Image Comics, Oni Press, 12 Gauge Comics, and Artisanal Media and he exhibits work internationally and nationally; most recently at Czong Institute for Contemporary Art (South Korea), the National Gallery of North Macedonia, and Shockboxx Gallery (California). His work has been featured in and recognized by international illustration competitions and art journals including "American Illustration," "Cheltenham Illustration Awards," "Creative Quarterly," "3x3," "Brightness Illustration Awards," "Coffin Bell Journal," "ArtAscent," and "Communication Arts." After earning his Masters of Fine Art (M.F.A.) in Sequential Art from Savannah College of Art and Design, Doug returned to his hometown near Nashville, TN with his wife and two children. Most days he can be found drawing, teaching, and perfecting his coffee brewing skills.
@dougdabbs

Susan's writing is mostly autobiographical. Formerly homeless,she now conducts writing workshops with women, the homeless, and the underserved founding "Pink Hanger Presents" to give voice to their stories.Susan is also an award winning photographer,capturing on 35mm film the internal beauty of women exposed. Her plays,films and photography have appeared in the Philadelphia Fringe Festival,in New York City, in Boston and Toronto.
Susan's poetry appeared in Sinister Wisdom,Corset Magazine,The Avocet, Spillway,Phila.Gay News."Laurel"coming-out memoir in the First Person Arts chapbook series,Art in the Time of Covid, Her memoir "Damaged" in "The Survivors Project".
A recipient of The Transformation Award from the Leeway Foundation, a co-recipient of The Art for Change Grant from the Leeway Foundation, is a 5- County Arts Fund co-recipient and received an honorarium from Philadelphia Fight for a memoir workshop for adults with HIV/AIDS which was presented at The Asian Arts Initiative as the performance piece "Shout".

KJ Williams is an abstract expressionist. She has studied art at Newbury College and The Art Institute of Boston before moving to New Hampshire. Through her work, KJ has expressed her physical pain from an accident in 1993 to the depression and frustration of trying to work while in pain. She has been compared to Frida Kahlo in that respect.
In the past few years, her paintings have leaned more towards abstract representation of her thoughts, causes, and passions.
'My work represents my life. It's who I am. It's my passion. If I could not express myself through my art, I would not exist.'
Her paintings, and drawings range from animals and people to abstract and self portraits. A piece can be dream orientated or a cause that she feels passionate about. Her strong use of earth tone colors capture a somewhat dark feel.
She has sold many of her works. She is one of the artists featured in The Pain Exhibit. Her work can also be seen at Deviant Art, and Artmajeur.

Bria Boecker grew up in Western Wisconsin and has loved books and writing from a young age. She's passionate about writing as a way to find magic in the everyday and to connect with other people. Currently, she's a senior attending the University of Wisconsin Madison and will be graduating with a degree in English Literature. She also loves spending time with friends and family, distance running, a good cup of coffee, and traveling. You can connect with her on Instagram @bookswithbria where she shares writing updates and what she's reading.

Like many ordinary Hong Kong people, KWONG Kwok Wai would describe his life as segmented into two periods: the Colonial rule and Chinese sovereignty. His artwork is all about reminiscing this historical phase.
Kwok Wai is a multi-disciplinary artist who focuses on painting and fiction writing. After serving in the journalistic field for nearly 30 years, witnessing and reporting the ups and downs of Hong Kong, he quitted his job as an Executive Producer in a TV news channel by the end of 2018 so that he could fully devote his time and attention to the pursuit of arts.
Through his work, Kwong explores the nature of human existence, his relationship with memories, the wider social environment and history. Real-life politics are utilized as raw materials to create fables in visual forms. Specific visual symbols are employed as metaphors to illustrate the politics-induced tremor inside as well as the entanglement. He has been drawing 'vines' for years to designate the process in which these political knots have become a part of him.
@kwongkwokwai

Brian Udall is a student working on his JD in environmental law. He was previously a contributor to SLUG magazine.

Lisa Cantwell is a recent graduate of the MFA in Writing program at the University of San Francisco. She is also a theatre director and educator living in Santa Monica, California.

Michael Baker is a writer and artist. He lives in San Diego, California.

Linda Schlossberg serves as Associate Director of the Women, Gender, and Sexuality Studies Program at Harvard University, where she teaches courses in literature and creative writing. She is the author of the novel Life in Miniature and the co-editor of Passing: Identity and Interpretation in Sexuality, Race, and Religion, and her work has appeared in a variety of publications, including McSweeney's, The Belladonna, Conduit, and Post Road. Schlossberg was the recipient of a 2019 Somerville Arts Council/ Mass Cultural Council Grant and the 2016 Emerging Writer Fellowship from the Writer's Center, and her feminist dystopic novel THE INCUBATOR is represented by Esmond Harmsworth of Aevitas Creative Management.

Sofie Rosalien Deen is a self-taught visual artist and writer with a background in Communications and Business Administration. She creates photograph series, paintings and poetry based on the subconscious. In September 2020 she created an exhibition based on her recently published poetry and photography book Raw., and is currently working on a photograph series that portray her dreams. Pieces from this serie will be exhibited in Spring 2021.
More information on her work can be found at:
www.instagram.com/sofierosalien
www.instagram.com/thegreatdanepoet
www.sofierosalien.store
www.sofierosalien.nl

Katie Kurtz received an M.A. in Visual & Critical Studies from California College of the Arts in San Francisco and a B.A. from Fairhaven College of Interdisciplinary Studies at Western Washington University in Bellingham. She lives in Seattle.

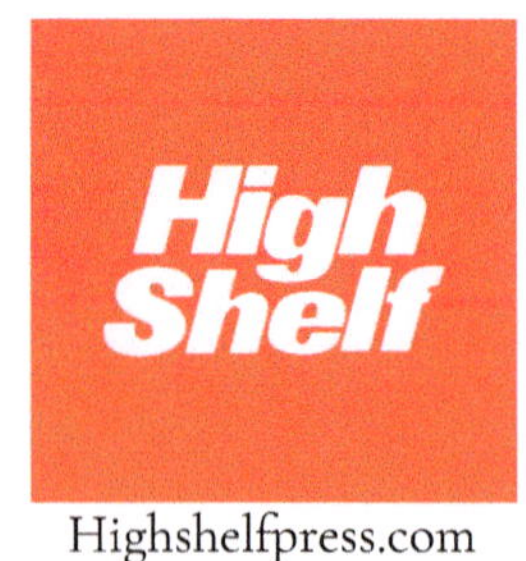

Highshelfpress.com

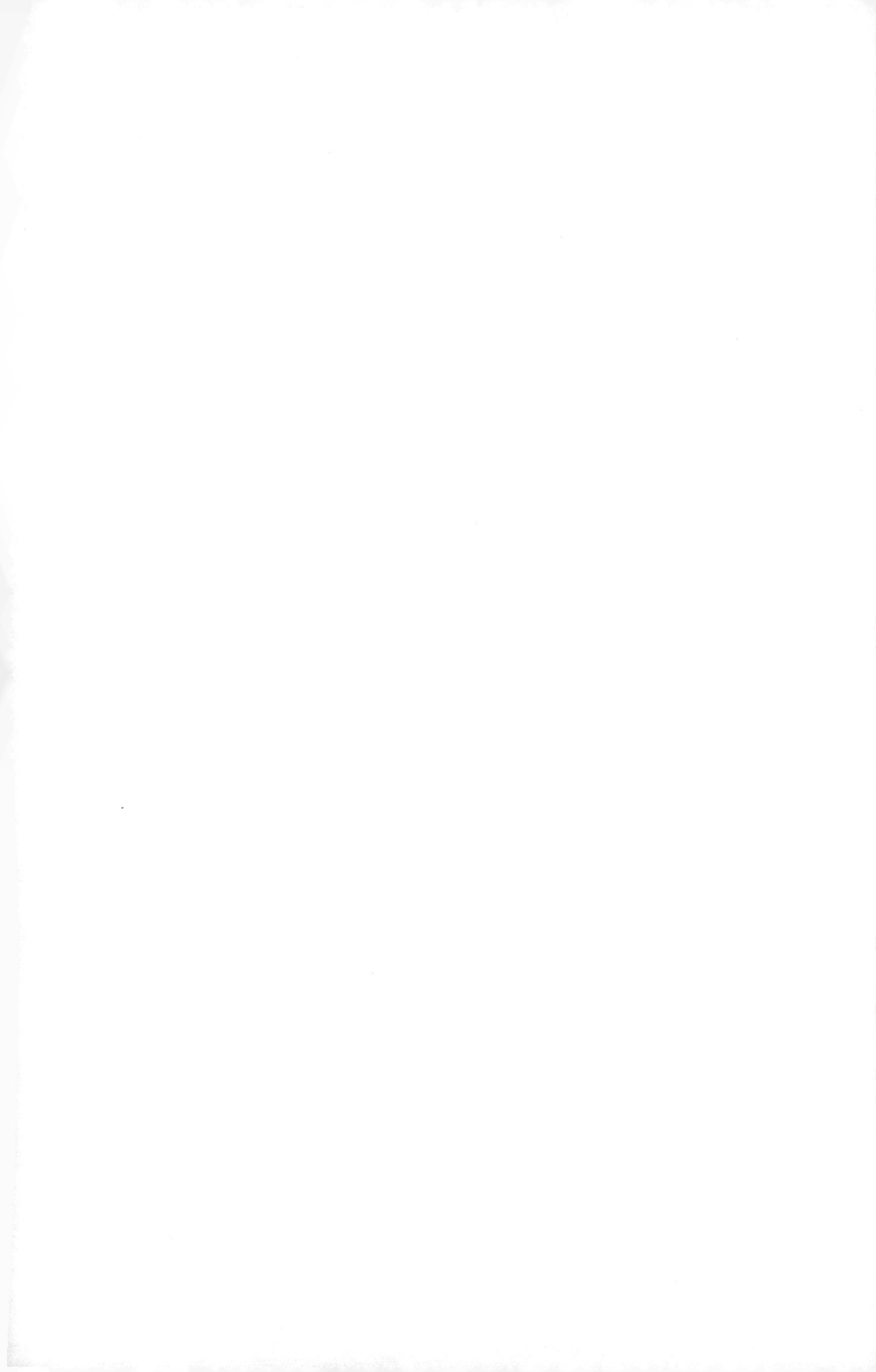